TRAINING AND CAREERS

for the

PROFESSIONAL MUSICIAN

by

GERALD McDONALD

GRESHAM BOOKS

First published in 1979 by

UNWIN BROTHERS
THE GRESHAM PRESS
OLD WOKING, SURREY
ENGLAND

ISBN 0 905418 03 4

Printed and bound in Great Britain by
UNWIN BROTHERS, THE GRESHAM PRESS,
OLD WOKING, SURREY, ENGLAND

Contents

List of Illustrations

Foreword

I AM OFTEN asked by young aspiring musicians about the qualifications needed for and the conditions to be expected in the life of a professional musician. Most of the answers to their questions will be found in Gerald McDonald's book for there is no one better able than he, with his long experience both as performer and administrator, to explain the complexities of a very mysterious profession.

I commend his book to enquiring youth and to all professional musicians as a comprehensive work of reference.

SIR CHARLES GROVES, CBE

Acknowledgements

For help, encouragement and advice:

Sir Charles Groves
Imogen Holst
David Jenkins
Hans Keller
Miranda de Grey
Anthony Friese Greene
George Mann
John May
John Pick
Eric Thompson
and my wife and family

and for use of photographs:

BBC Photograph Library
National Youth Orchestra
Royal Military School of Music
Director, South Bank Concert Halls
London Symphony Orchestra
Yorkshire Post
Snape Maltings Foundation
Nigel Luckhurst
G. Macdominic

Introduction

'THEY LAUGHED WHEN I sat down at the piano but they all listened in amazement when I started to play.' So ran the advertisement familiar in the 1930s for 'learning the piano in ten easy lessons', the implication being that there is a painless, magic formula for acquiring expertise. But to achieve success in any field, and especially in music, talent and aptitude must be reinforced by enthusiasm, dedication and sustained hard work.

However the piano-teaching methods of the thirties did enable many people to 'play a little' and taught them the basic elements of notation and form. Mention of them reminds us that in those days nearly every home had a piano, no matter how many notes were missing or stuck, or even if it was permanently flat or out of tune. Many homes indeed had a harmonium as well and, round the keyboard of one or the other, family and friends gathered on a Sunday evening to sing the latest hits from the shows: *The New Moon* ('Lover come back to me') or *The Desert Song* ('One alone'); the newest dance tunes—'Ain't she sweet?' and ''Bye, 'bye, blackbird'; famous ballads such as 'Because' and, of course, choruses from the *Messiah* and *Elijah* and the ever popular Gilbert and Sullivan operas. At whatever level, most people could join in and a very large number could take charge of the proceedings at the piano.

Those days of participation in home music seemed until recently to have gone forever, switched off permanently by the radio, the television and the hi-fi set. But miraculously there are signs of a revival in private music-making as a result of determined and devoted work carried out in various educational fields since the war. Pianos, new and old, are in demand again. So are domestic organs, and even harpsichords and clavichords. Violins, violas and cellos, and the bows for them, are in such short supply that thousands are imported from Hong Kong and Japan; and our own colleges of instrument making and repairing (keyboard, wind instrument and strings), such as Newark Technical College and the Instrument Making Department at the ILEA London College of Furniture, are flourishing.

Paradoxically, the influence of radio and television, and various forms of recorded music, has probably been an important factor in this revival of interest. The use of the harpsichord, flute and recorder in the introductory music of a popular television series; musical quiz programmes; the ready availability of recorded classics; and even the introduction of excerpts from the music of Bach, Beethoven, Brahms and others into the Pop world have helped re-awaken interest in music as a general, rather than as an intellectual, pleasure.

The revival of a general interest in music and music-making is marvellous, but there is a wide difference between the standard of proficiency and degree of aptitude required to give real pleasure in instrumental playing or singing at a recreational level and the great talent and expertise needed for success in a professional career.

Nothing written in this book is meant to discourage the gifted amateur; indeed it might be said that the musical health of any country depends on the continuing growth of a strong amateur movement. The hundreds of brass bands and choral societies which achieve remarkable musical standards, and groups run by the Rural Music Schools give immense stimulation and satisfaction to thousands of players and singers. But a strong amateur growth needs strong professional backing and it is not always easy for the parents of the musically gifted children, who are destined to be the next generation of professional musicians, to know what to do about their training.

The aim of this book is to provide an introductory guide to the various branches of the music profession for students, parents and teachers, and perhaps also for professional musicians who are interested in branches of music other than their own. For parents and students alike, there can be no short cuts, no easy methods; just a long, hard and expensive preparation and training for a demanding profession. But music is a profession in which the rewards in terms of satisfaction and pleasure given are scarcely to be equalled in any other field.

SECTION I

Preparing for a Career

SCHOOL YEARS

SPOTTING THE TALENT

DESPITE THE UNDOUBTED renaissance of general interest in music in Britain, we are still a long way from being a musical nation. We have in general, a national attitude to music which fosters an unenthusiastic, undiscriminating general environment, inhibiting the possibility of music being absorbed by babies and very young children as a natural part of their daily life. A child growing up in an environment in which music is a normal occupation and pleasure has a chance of becoming as familiar with the taste and flavour of music as with the basic elements of letters and words for reading and writing. Apart from the families of musicians themselves, this background is quite exceptional in Britain.

The Japanese, whose absorption of Western skills in all fields is so thorough, have demonstrated this thoroughness in the manner of their adoption of Western music over the past fifty years. In the Suzuki violin method, for example, the key factor is that the mother must take lessons in the method before the child begins to learn, so that the mother is always several months ahead of the child and thus sets the right atmosphere in the home for practice, without which no lessons can be effective. There may be some aspects of the Suzuki method which are controversial, but as proof of its effectiveness every major orchestra in Europe and the United States now has a large quota of Japanese string players, several indeed are the leaders of famous orchestras. Japan has also produced such outstanding soloists as Mayumi Fujikawa and Masuko Ushioda.

An early recognition of musical skill is absolutely vital; if a child has potential talent it needs to be carefully nurtured from the beginning. Early teaching is crucial, at six or seven years of age for string players and pianists and at ten or eleven for wind and brass instrumentalists. An early start is desirable too for the development of the ears and senses of any children displaying musical awareness, no matter what instruments they may later take up, or how their voices may develop. A dictum concerning the religious life used to be attributed to the Jesuits: 'Give us a boy before he is seven and we'll have him for life.' So it is with the formation and establishment of habits of mind and body. Habits of tonal and rythmic sense, habits of posture, technique and style, once acquired and set, are there for life. Later teaching may modify or enhance them, but they become virtually impossible to change fundamentally once they are set. The great violinist, David Oistrakh, after hearing the highly promising seven-year-old son of a British diplomat in Moscow, remarked: 'What a pity he didn't come to me sooner—it is already too late.'

The first signs of musical interest in very young children is the pleasure they take in musical sounds of all kinds, and their attempts to reproduce them in rhythm and tune by beating, singing, pretending to play an instrument, or touching the notes of a piano if there is one in the house. All this is very common and does not denote any particular latent talent unless it grows into a more marked interest in which certain types of melody or patterns of rhythm start to occupy a child's attention as a regular source of interest and pleasure.

In a musical family, of course, it is likely that the mother will encourage the child to try to sing or to play whatever instruments are to hand—piano, pipes or recorders, or toy fiddles and drums. Early lessons will be given or arranged and a start will have been made. For musical children of a non-musical family the first guidance will probably come at school—a discerning teacher may notice a child's interest in, and wish to imitate, sounds, and may then give encouragement and help.

At about the age of five or six it should be apparent if a child has the kind of interest in and flair for making music that justify formal instrumental lessons. The next three steps are the parental decision to pay for such lessons, buying an instrument and finding a good teacher, all of which may pose problems. At this stage it is still difficult to say that there is anything there but some talent. How much talent, and where it might lead, depend on these three problems being resolved and upon the child's real gifts and growth under the stimulus of lessons. It may be possible to solve these problems entirely at school, but the provision and level of teaching varies widely between the local education authorities and individual schools, and private lessons may be essential. The future of a potential professional may be permanently made or marred at this stage.

Early instrumental and theory music lessons should be short—say fifteen or twenty minutes each once a week, leading up to thirty minutes. Most good teachers will arrange pro rata fees for these short lessons, but, of course, good lessons will not be cheap. There really is no reason to think that music teachers should be paid less than any other skilled person in any craft or art: after all teaching is a branch of the profession the child himself may later take up. The Incorporated Society of Musicians recommends minimum rates for the members of its Teachers Section, but, of course, many well-known teachers charge several times the recommended figure. On the other hand the Music Teachers Association reports the average fees charged as being lower.

It is essential to get expert advice on buying an instrument. There are cheap instruments to be obtained, but on no account should they be bought without advice or just because they are cheap. They must be of the right pitch, capable of being tuned accurately and, since music is concerned with a pleasant sound and early associations are of prime importance for a student, the instrument must have a good tone. It is worthwhile spending a few more pounds on a violin and on a decent bow to ensure that good effects can be obtained, or on an iron-framed piano of correct pitch with all its notes working and even in quality, and it is vital to get woodwind instruments made to modern concert pitch; there are many high-pitch ones around, so beware!

Getting a teacher can prove quite a problem; the really good ones are in great demand. Most professional musicians find it difficult to teach their own children beyond a certain point and they too will be looking for an outside teacher. Their advantage is that they know where to look for someone suitable. Not every teacher, however good, will suit every child—and vice versa. Perhaps there will be someone you know, a friend of the family or of the school teacher; perhaps you will see an advertisement (although many people believe that really good teachers are so besieged by applicants for lessons that they seldom need to advertise, except for the purpose of keeping their names before the public in a general sense), or you may have someone recommended by another parent. Whatever the method of introduction it is wise to arrange an introductory lesson to see if teacher and child like each other.

Once started the parents' job is to ensure that practice is done regularly and accurately—many teachers write down the tasks for the week in a little notebook to remind child and parent alike what is required for the next lesson. Practice should not be made a drudge or a bore, but firmness and encouragement are needed at all levels and all ages. Actually five, ten, or fifteen minutes of real concentration are worth hours of desultory or mechanical work which often degenerates into repeating the same mistakes over and over again, leading to a going back rather than forward.

One of the most cheering post-war developments in general education has been the introduction of instrumental lessons at school, often by peripatetic visiting teachers, usually outside the school curriculum in free time and mostly by group teaching methods. However, the provision of such facilities greatly depends on whether the Head is musically inclined, whether the local education authority puts up the money—this varies widely from authority to authority and from area to area—and whether instruments are provided on loan. Enthusiastic heads have worked miracles in many unpromising districts and schools, resulting in turn in many children taking up music and providing really enjoyable school concerts at Christmas and parents' days. When there is co-operation with the drama departments and with woodwork and metal departments (for making instruments) some remarkable results have been achieved in districts which might on the surface appear unpromising and with children whose interest might otherwise never have been aroused.

For the purposes of potential professionals, however, even these relatively rare successes must be regarded as an introduction to music and a stimulus to greater individual effort and personal lessons, rather than as an end in themselves. String class lessons, where several children learn together, have the advantage of teaching children to play with others, but the drawback is that pursuit of individual standards may sometimes be sacrificed to the slowest member. There is, however, one further major advantage with class instrumental teaching—the children are often entered in class or group events at music festivals, and there, in competition with children from many different schools and family backgrounds, they get their first taste of performance, of comparing standards, and of enhanced interest through the feeling of belonging to a much larger musical community. The main thing is that the young potential should be recognised and that the music teacher in the school should collaborate fully with the parents in arranging for the child to have the best possible individual lessons.

All manner of strains and stresses are set up, for the school teacher as well as for the child, by the demands of practice. Most really talented children will be learning two instruments; if their main one is the piano they should also learn a melodic one, string or wind, to develop their sense of continuity, cantabile and melody; and if the main one is a melodic instrument, they should learn the piano for a sense of harmony and general musicianship. Many great string players, such as Rostropovitch, are fine pianists also. Talented children will also have theory lessons for the recurring Associated Board[1] or other exams in progressive grades, giving a basic understanding of melody, harmony and structure in music.

Some children will take music as a curriculum subject at school leading to 'O' and 'A' level examinations, but these concern the history and appreciation of music rather than music-making, and there is as yet no way of taking an 'O' or 'A' level in performance. There is a move to institute performance examinations, parallel perhaps to the oral examinations in fluency in the use of modern languages.

For musical children, however bright they may be academically, either homework or practice is liable to suffer once they get to the stage of having to spend one or two hours, or even more, a day on instrumental practice. The same is true of their participation in games,[2] in fact some sports liable to damage the fingers or hands, like hockey, may be banned altogether. The sympathy and intelligent help of class teachers, therefore, is crucial in enabling the young musician to make the most of his school years without either becoming overwhelmed or being left out of normal school life.

A development strongly supported in the Gulbenkian 1977 report on musical

---

[1]The Associated Board of the Royal Schools of Music

[2]Interviewed by *Annabel* magazine Jacqueline du Pre declared: 'When I was ten I won a scholarship which paid for my musical education but it demanded a lot of practice, which I loathed. Consequently my ordinary study time was eaten into...'

education is that of music centres or 'houses' attached to comprehensive schools (Pimlico is an outstanding example). Musically gifted children are able to enjoy specialist teaching in company with others, but without losing the benefit of 'belonging' to the general school.

Some, of course, favour conditions at specialist schools, such as the Yehudi Menuhin School in Sussex or Chethams Hospital School in Manchester, where the emphasis is on music, although a general education is also given. Such schools provide mutual stimulation for gifted children, time for individual practice, performance opportunities, and orchestra, choir and chamber music as part of the curriculum—in short music as part of the curriculum and not crammed into the dinner hour or play time.

There are mixed opinions among experts on the efficacy of these special schools and on the advisability of emphasis. Everything depends on the quality of specialist and general staff. In recent years the Menuhin School has produced such outstanding young soloists as Nigel Kennedy (violin), Colin Carr (cello) and Elizabeth Perry (violin).

Whatever the opinions, there are few places available and the cost is beyond most parents. Not many education authorities or private scholarship trusts are willing to commit themselves for several years to a continuing bill of such magnitude.

There are also many public schools which offer generous open music scholarships; they are well worth examining carefully, bearing in mind the need for expert musical tuition and for a stimulating general school musical activity to match the indisputable advantages of the general education there.

The famous choir schools are mainly connected with cathedrals and collegiate churches and the boys sing the daily services. There is great value to be gained from the discipline of singing, and a superb repertoire from which to draw knowledge and experience of music. Among the best-known choir schools are Westminster, St Paul's and, of course, King's College Chapel, Cambridge. There are also facilities at many choir schools for learning instruments as well as the provision of a general education.

It is one thing to emphasise the necessity for a really good teacher from the earliest age for the potential professional, but the big question is how to find one. Easy, it may be said, if one lives in London, or in Liverpool, Glasgow, Birmingham, Bournemouth or Manchester, where resident symphony orchestras provide a large pool of professional instrumental teachers, mostly with wives and children who are also experienced professional musicians, and only too glad to take pupils of all ages—but it is quite another thing to find one in smaller towns and in the vast rural areas of East Anglia, Cumbria, the West Country and most of Scotland and Wales.

Consequently, many children have to undertake long journeys every Saturday to their nearest big centre to get their weekly private lessons and to take part in music group activities, orchestras, etc., run by associations of local teachers, or by the local education authority. These Saturday groups are also organised by the junior schools of the main music colleges in big cities (see Appendix 4) and by private music schools in many localities. There is, however, no uniformity of provision or standard, and although they and the Rural Music Schools do wonderful work in many country areas, much depends on the scale of financial support given by the local education authority and on the personality and ability of the individual director and teachers.

One last general word about teachers. It is a common mistake to think in terms of absolutes. The teacher's role at every age and every stage is twofold—first to impart certain basic facts of music and of technique, and secondly to draw out the pupil's talent along lines of development most suited to his or her physical, intellectual and artistic individuality. The teacher must combine firmness with adaptability and imagination.

While it is futile to keep changing one's teacher under the fond but illusory belief that somewhere there is someone who will really make one great, it can be a good idea to change teachers at certain stages. There comes a moment when new impetus and stimulation are required—it isn't just a question of 'better', there is a virtue in 'different' and many teachers feel this as acutely as do their students. Holst once said 'The last and most difficult thing for a teacher to learn is not to become, or believe he is, indispensable to the pupil.'

Appendix I contains a list of specialist schools and schools offering music facilities and scholarships.

ASSOCIATED BOARD AND OTHER EXAMINATIONS

ONE OF THE best ways of measuring a student's development and progress is by means of the external examinations sponsored by the organisations listed below. They may be taken by students from any part of the country, who do not have to be enrolled at any of the colleges concerned. The examinations, in singing, pianoforte, all instruments, and theory and harmony (as well as speech and drama in many cases), are held regularly in several main centres at home and abroad. The Associated Board of the Royal Schools of Music have eight grades—a proper *Gradus ad Parnassum* to the stage of entering a college of music as a full-time student or of taking an external diploma, eg. LRAM or ARCM. Graded examinations are also arranged by the Guildhall School of Music and Drama, the London College of Music, and Trinity College of Music, London, on a national and world-wide basis, and they too can lead to acceptance as a full-time music student, or to the taking of the appropriate external diploma.

Examinations have their critics and, indeed, exams do not necessarily tell the whole story. But they do have certain merits: as a stimulus for students—something they have got to work for in a graded and disciplined way;

as an experience of performing to a critical audience in the form of the examiner; as a reminder to teachers of the comprehensive nature of their task and as a means of gauging their own success with their pupils; these and many other benefits are positive gains far outweighing any disadvantage the critics may cite.

It is, for instance, asserted that the students play, or sing, below their best because they are nervous. Every performer, even the most experienced and famous, is nervous before performing (or should be). Only those who learn how to cope with this condition can hope to become professional musicians in any area of performance.

The addresses of the bodies organising external examinations at this level are:

ASSOCIATED BOARD OF THE ROYAL SCHOOLS OF MUSIC
(Royal Academy of Music, Royal College of Music, Royal Northern College of Music, Royal Scottish Academy of Music & Drama)
14 Bedford Square, London WC1B 3JG;

GUILDHALL SCHOOL OF MUSIC & DRAMA
John Carpenter Street, Victoria Embankment, London EC4Y 0AR;

LONDON COLLEGE OF MUSIC EXAMINATIONS
47 Gt Marlborough Street, London W1V 2AS;

TRINITY COLLEGE OF MUSIC, LONDON
11 Mandeville Place, London W1M 6AQ.

FESTIVALS AND COMPETITIONS

FESTIVALS HAVE ALREADY been mentioned briefly. Here, too, as with examinations, teachers hold strong, opposing views about festivals, competitive or otherwise. Some find the element of pot-hunting, of being a 'little show-off', unbearable aesthetically and degrading for pupils and teachers alike. Music, they feel, should be performed for its own sake by the young, not for ephemeral admiration or for rewards.

Others, no less sincerely, believe that such events are an essential early introduction to what the music profession is really like—hard and competitive—and that one has to be a show-off to dare to perform in public at all, to do so with diffidence or excessive modesty would be ineffectual and certain to prove calamitous in a career. Similar opinions apply to important international competitions, and are discussed later.

There are hundreds of festivals in all parts of the country, some organised by or in conjunction with local authorities, but many, perhaps most, organised by enthusiastic volunteers as a labour of love and service.

A full list of music festivals can be obtained from:

THE BRITISH FEDERATION OF MUSIC FESTIVALS
106 Gloucester Place, London W1H 3DB.

The Federation incorporates the Music Teachers Association and provides a
regular bulletin of information and advice about fees, repertoire and many other
relevant matters, invaluable to teachers and organisers alike.

YOUTH ORCHESTRAS

AT THE SCHOOL stage youth orchestras provide one of the most encouraging
developments on our national scene for young musicians. Parallel with the
splendid efforts of the indefatigable Sir Robert Mayer to provide opportunities
for young people to attend concerts and opera by leading professional orchestras
and companies, through his Youth and Music Organisation (his own very British
adaptation of the continental *Jeunnesses Musicales*), many opportunities have
been provided for young musicians to perform together.

Most big towns and districts have their own youth orchestras, organised by
the local education authorities, which rehearse regularly, have holiday courses
and give concerts, even going on foreign tours. Many are run in conjunction
with the Saturday music courses at local centres. They offer the young student
an opportunity of playing with the best players among his or her local contemporaries, and a chance of meeting his fellows from all walks of life.

This is especially true of the National Youth Orchestra, which has three
courses a year during the Christmas, Easter and summer holidays. The Musical
Director hears a vast number of applicants, literally thousands, at auditions in
many different centres all over the country, from whom some 150 to 175 are
chosen to take part in the courses. The courses and the ensuing concerts, which
include appearances at the Royal Festival Hall, Fairfield Hall, Croydon, and
at the BBC Royal Albert Hall Proms, are conducted by distinguished international conductors, with sectional coaching by the best orchestral players in the
land.

Those chosen have to pay a fee for attending these residential courses, but in
most cases grants are made by the local education authorities concerned, and in
special cases the National Youth Orchestra has bursary funds of its own to
assist the needy student. Some local youth orchestras have instruments of their
own to lend to students, and other facilitate loans from 'friends'.

The recently formed European Community Youth Orchestra aims to recruit
the cream of young talent to play under famous conductors: Claudio Abbado,
Maazel and others. Mr Edward Heath, who gave much support to the formation
of the orchestra, also exercised his musical skills by conducting part of their
inaugural programme.

The National Youth Orchestra of Great Britain rehearsing with Pierre Boulez.

The address of the British office is:

EUROPEAN COMMUNITY YOUTH ORCHESTRA
24 Cadogan Square, London SW1X 0JP.

A list of the main national youth orchestras and the address of the National Association of Youth Orchestras is given in Appendix 2.

SUMMER SCHOOLS AND HOLIDAY COURSES

IN ADDITION TO the many holiday courses run by the various youth orchestras, there is a large number of summer schools and residential holiday courses. Several are run by the local authorities, but most are organised by a variety of groups of enthusiasts, some on behalf of official organisations—the Music Teachers Association (at Downe House), the Rural Music Schools Association

Sir Peter Pears taking a master class in opera at Snape Maltings. The soprano is Hilary Straw who is now working with the National Opera Studio.

and the Ernest Read Music Association for instance—and some by individual teachers or groups of teachers like the Kato Havas Violin Schools in spring and summer and Yfrah Neaman's Summer Violin School at Hengrave Hall in Suffolk. Probably the one best known to the general public is Dartington Summer School directed by Sir William Glock, where hundreds of people of all ages, from young children to very senior enthusiasts indeed, amateurs and distinguished professionals, students and teachers, attend one or more of the three weeks there. They make music at every level, attend master classes by some of the world's finest musicians and hear them give recitals, and above all they get the immense reassurance of feeling a sense of 'belonging' to the wider community of musicians in the mutual giving and receiving of experience and stimulation.

Each of these holiday courses has its own specialities and flavours. Some concentrate on orchestral playing, others on piano repertoire, oratorio, opera, church music, conducting, old instruments, folk music or organ music. Wavendon Allmusic Plan presided over by Johnny Dankworth and Cleo Laine specialises in composition and improvisation; the Snape Maltings courses cater for master classes in performance for post-graduate and advanced students under the guidance of Peter Pears, and the International Festival Seminar at Prussia Cove in Cornwall. Many courses are devoted solely to chamber music, and at all of them string quartets and quintets play a big part, often continuing long into the night and through to the next morning.

Although summer schools are referred to here in the context of school life, they are a source of recreation and refreshment to students from colleges and universities too, also to teachers, soloists, orchestral players, and mums and dads in the widest spectrum of ages, tastes and degrees of expertise. They provide something for everyone, with fine recitals by leading musicians, opportunities for learning, for playing, for accompanists to practice, for professionals to catch the enthusiasm of the amateurs, and for all to make contacts and friends. The atmosphere at summer schools is distinctly heady; being there is not 'real life' but they offer a fine tonic and stimulant to the participants in preparation for their return to everyday life.

In addition to the many summer schools held regularly in Britain there are also many others in many parts of Europe and in the United States. A list of them with the names and addresses of the Secretaries appears in the *British Music Yearbook*. Full details of all the courses in Britain are given in the February issue of the *Music Teacher* every year.

Preparing for a Career

ADVANCED TRAINING

THE BIG MOMENT of decision comes at the point of leaving school when a choice has to be made between the various alternatives available for advanced training. Most types of full-time advanced music study at university, music college or college of education (teachers training) call for students of at least eighteen years of age (by December in the academic year in which they start). There are also varying minimum requirements of general educational standard at school leaving age; each institution has its own, but the lowest demand is for at least five passes at 'O' level. Those who decide that the world of professional performance is not for them will also be influenced in their choice of further training by their results in 'O' and 'A' level examinations. There are several options open to them: as teachers, composers, musicologists and critics, in the important new field of administration, in the fascinating area of instrument making and repairing, as well as careers in radio, television, commercial recording and technology.

PRE-COLLEGE COURSES

FOR THOSE WHO want to leave school at, say, sixteen and who want more general musical education than they can get, or afford to pay for, by having private lessons, there are a number of useful pre-college music courses to which entry can be made at sixteen. Most of them include a principal and a second instrument study, plus theory, harmony, history and other courses which will have to be taken at a more intensive level in their post-eighteen courses. These intermediate courses usually last for two years. Preparation for 'A' level examinations is also offered.

A list of pre-college courses is given in Appendix 3.

MAIN MUSIC COLLEGES

THE DECISION CONCERNING the type of advanced training eventually to be undertaken will probably have been made before leaving school, at whatever age that occurs. For some students the way ahead will be clear. There are several indications of special performance gifts which will make the particular choice of advanced training inevitable, for instance: early brilliance as an instrumentalist, with regular high distinction marks in Associated Board exams up to grade eight; solo performances with one of the youth orchestras, or even with one of the professional orchestras; or personal adoption by one of the master teachers. A few of these very gifted students may decide on private tuition with a master teacher outside the orbit of one of the colleges of music. They will need exceptional dedication, assiduity and self-discipline; they will also need money from some private source to compensate for their ineligibility for a mandatory grant for further training at a recognised institution. They will forfeit the daily stimulus derived from working among their contemporary peers and they will require inspired guidance from teachers, parents and professional friends to stimulate them into hearing other performers and reflecting upon other arts and ideas. In return they may expect a high concentration of quality teaching.

The majority of these born performers, however, will go to one of the colleges of music where they will rub shoulders and talents with the best of their contempories. Some of them will have been attending one of the colleges in the junior school and may have been marked out for entry into the college proper on reaching the age of eighteen. Others will have been taking the Associated Board examinations or those of other colleges up to the grade qualifying for entry and the possibility of scholarships. The competition for places is very keen indeed and applicants need to have a good general educational background to support their musical talents in order to gain admission.

THE ROYAL ACADEMY OF MUSIC, founded in 1822, takes 650 full-time students in its handsome 1910 buildings in the Marylebone Road, London, and it has a fine new addition in the Jack Lyons Concert Hall and Theatre. (York University owes its splendid Music Centre and Concert Hall to Sir Jack Lyons also.) The Royal Academy's Licentiate diploma is open to external as well as to internal students; the GRSM (Graduate of the Royal Schools of Music) may be taken internally; either a teacher's or a performer's LRAM may be taken. Associates and Fellows (ARAM and FRAM) are honorary awards to distinguished former students.

THE ROYAL COLLEGE OF MUSIC was one of the many splendid artistic enterprises developed under the auspices of Prince Albert after the highly successful Exhibition of 1851. It, too, has an imposing home in Prince Consort Road, London SW7, behind the Royal Albert Hall, with a student enrolment of 650. It possesses a fine collection of early instruments. The Royal College does not offer a Licentiate diploma, but its Associate diploma is open to external as well as internal students, and its Fellows are elected; the GRSM may be taken internally.

TRINITY COLLEGE OF MUSIC, LONDON, is an earlier foundation, dating from 1872 and owns a small but very valuable property in Mandeville Place, London W1, not far from Oxford Street. Trinity has about 400 full-time students and some part-time students. It operates a world-wide examination system and its Licentiate and Fellowship diplomas are open to external as well as internal students; but its graduate diploma GTCL is open to internal students only.

THE GUILDHALL SCHOOL OF MUSIC AND DRAMA, 1880, sponsored by the city of London, has moved into new purpose-built premises in the Barbican—the first occupants of the Barbican Arts Centre, designed to house in addition the Royal Shakespeare Company, the London Symphony Orchestra, a cinema, art gallery and library. There are 400 full-time students and a large number of part-time students at the Guildhall, and internal and external examinations are offered for the Licentiate (LGSM). The Associate (AGSM) diploma is available to those taking the full three-year full-time course, as is the GGSM for graduate students, and the Fellowship is an honorary distinction.

THE LONDON COLLEGE OF MUSIC is a private school, again with small but very valuable premises in Great Marlborough Street, off Regent Street, London W1. There are some 200 students; its diplomas (ALCM, LLCM, FLCM) are open to external and internal students; its GLCM and LLCM (school music) are only open to internal students.

THE ROYAL NORTHERN COLLEGE OF MUSIC was formed by the amalgamation of the Royal Manchester College of Music (one of Charles Hallé's inspired enterprises in Manchester) and the Northern School of Music (one of the last of the major private schools linked to the important work of the famous piano teacher, Tobias Matthay). Planned from the outset by the governing bodies of both institutions with four major local authorites—Lancashire, Cheshire, Manchester and Salford—the Royal Northern College now occupies the splendid new purpose-built college in Oxford Road, near to Manchester city centre. A basic four-year course gives it an important advantage over the other colleges, and because of its close financial links with the local authorities the Royal Northern College is able to provide advanced training for the students, and conditions of work for its professional staff far more rewarding and secure than those obtaining in London, for example. The diplomas are open to internal students only. The GRSM may be taken.

THE ROYAL SCOTTISH ACADEMY OF MUSIC, the second senior college dating back to 1847, caters for about 250 students and its diploma is awarded to internal students only. The Royal Scottish Academy enjoys a direct grant from the Scottish Department of Education and is also able to provide better and more secure conditions than most other colleges.

THE BIRMINGHAM SCHOOL OF MUSIC offers its Associate diploma to external as well as to internal students, reserving graduate status for internal award only. The school occupies new premises in the city centre as an integral part of the City of Birmingham Polytechnic.

All these colleges offer facilities for acquiring graduate status with a view to careers as teachers. They all have a large number of internal scholarships at their disposal. Most of these scholarships are not large; £150 is the maximum, to protect the holders from the loss of any part of a DES grant for which they may be qualified. The colleges also have access to various special pockets and private patrons from whom help may be obtained for students ineligible for an official grant, or in exceptional need.

Marvels have been done by the colleges for many years with slender and insecure means, but as a result of inflation, high maintenance costs of buildings, and day-to-day running costs, the struggle for survival on an independent basis is becoming more and more difficult. Few would assert that conditions are as they should be in modern terms and current world excellence in music, or in comparison with the facilities available to students and the conditions of work and pay offered to staff in universities, polytechnics and other institutions of higher education in Britain.

Students at the colleges of music will have a rather restricted sort of campus life—not a bit like that enjoyed at university—their attendance at college being limited to one, or at best two, periods of one hour on their principal instrument per week, one shorter period on their second study, and two periods on theory and harmony in its various aspects. If they play an orchestral instrument there may be a weekly orchestral rehearsal; there may be opera or choral rehearsals. And that is about the extent of official and corporate activities—scarcely seven hours a week at best. This is mainly because the colleges of music do not enjoy direct grants from education authorities and receive only limited deficiency grants. This inhibits their ability to develop their courses and improve conditions for students, as, depending for their income upon students' fees, they have to accept several times more in numbers than their buildings and other facilities are geared to cope with.

In 1965 and again in 1977 the Gulbenkian Reports on the training of musicians emphasised the fact that the London colleges had tended to remain outside the mainstream of further and higher education, resulting in a high price being paid for semi-independence.

The Reports recommend that the method of financing the colleges from public funds should be changed to enable them to reduce the student level from 650 each at the Royal Academy of Music and Royal College of Music to about 400; to increase the individual 'first study' to two hours a week; to increase the rates of pay of professors, many of whom in 1977 were earning less than music teachers in schools; to recognise the differing needs of performers, instrumental

teachers and class teachers and to arrange the courses accordingly to be of
different emphases and durations; to improve career advice which should grow
out of tutorials with as much 'in-service' training as can be arranged with
professional bodies and the Union. It is also suggested that these changes can
best be achieved by bringing all London colleges (except the Guildhall School
of Music and Drama) into the public sector, with the Royal Academy of Music
and the Royal College of Music becoming monotechnics or colleges of London
University.

The Reports also point out the benefits already enjoyed by students at the
Royal Scottish Academy of Music, financed directly by the Scottish Education
Department, and at the Royal Northern College of Music since its reconstitution
and the adoption of both methods similar to those advocated here for the London
colleges.

Of course the keen and intelligent students organise all manner of activities
(chamber music groups, recitals and concerts) outside their colleges and their
curriculum schedules, and in doing so they get much support and encouragement
from their professors. But the limitations are serious, especially in terms of travel
costs, suitable meeting places for playing together, and accommodation generally.
By no means least is the handicap for the more reticent, shy students who may
easily get left out of the general swim of music-making groups, overshadowed
by their more extrovert colleagues. Many a musician can look back with
amazement at the number of brilliant, much envied star students of their own
times who have faded into oblivion, whilst their less glamorous contemporaries
are now making excellent careers as leaders, principals and soloists.

One type of performer for whom the decision about further training is very
difficult is the singer, and more especially the male singer. A few professional
singers develop out of the world of boys in choir schools, where they are taught
the rudiments of music. Most male singers, however, do not discover that they
have a voice worth cultivating until they are in their twenties, and even then
they have the added disadvantage that the pitch of the male voice does not finally
settle until the age of thirty-three; usually it rises, so that basses at twenty-four
become bass-baritones at thirty-three. Many of these singers have had no musical
training or background at all; no knowledge of reading music, of pitch, key
harmony, structure or form. They are in the position of someone who finds a
genuine Strad or Amati or Guanerius in the attic (I stress *genuine* because most
such 'finds' are awful factory-made copies) and has no idea how to use it
properly; it can make a beautiful sound, but it needs years of work to release
its potential.

To give up a career, work and income in the mid-twenties is no light decision
to take. It is very hard indeed to get an official grant from TOPS (Training
Opportunities Scheme) for a change of employment, because it may well prove
in the long run that the training does not lead to any employment, as a singer
at any rate. The private scholarship trusts are stretched to their limits by

hundreds of such applications and it may be imperative to move away from one's home town to get the expert coaching and advice required. For an absolute beginner all the associated skills must be learned from scratch—reading music, harmony, acquaintance with the immense repertoire of operatic, choral and orchestral music, and knowledge of languages such as Italian, German and French—all essential equipment for the professional singer.

For single men the situation is fraught enough, but not desperate; for married men with children the difficulties are daunting. But determination, inspired advice from someone in the profession with vision, dedication from a devoted wife (many have to keep the roof over the husband's head by becoming the main breadwinner during these difficult years) can prevail and have often done so. Frank Titterton, for example, was an engineer, and John Shirley-Quirk, a former schoolmaster in Liverpool had for inspiration that splendid teacher, Austen Carnegie (who, incidentally, despite only having one arm, could play the accompaniments of Brahms and Schubert Lieder in special arrangements with his one hand!).

Female singers are more fortunate in that they can, and do, start singing at a much earlier age. Their problem may be said to be the opposite to that of the men—namely that they learn to sing 'prettily' when young and develop habits of production which may inhibit their blossoming fully in their twenties, when they should be growing into more mature and dramatic styles of singing. But the great advantage they have is that, through starting young, they usually have a general musical education and background. There are, nevertheless, late developers among female singers too; the most notable in the forties was Kathleen Ferrier, who entered a music festival in the piano class and put her name down also in the contralto class 'for fun'. She was at the time a telephone operator.

The development of opera departments at the music colleges, notably those offering advanced study at the Royal Northern College of Music in Manchester and at the Royal Academy of Music, the Royal College of Music and the Guildhall School of Music and Drama in London, is an important new factor in the training of young opera singers. Much of the advanced student work undertaken by the London Opera Centre until 1978 can now be handled by the colleges, and the newly set-up National Opera Studio will concentrate on the training of young professionals, in close association with the major opera companies. With the Welsh National Opera, Scottish Opera, Glyndebourne Touring Opera and the exciting prospects of an English National Opera based in Leeds as well as in London, together with the Royal Opera House and Glyndebourne Festival Opera, all functioning fully, the opportunities and prospects for professional singers, including late developers, have improved greatly.

The music colleges also provide training for potential teachers, that is music teachers in schools; indeed it is asserted by some critics that the whole grant system is mainly directed to this end, resulting in courses and emphasis geared less to excellence in performance than to general musicianship of a more academic kind. The colleges offer diplomas in performing and in teaching (individual private teaching as well as class teaching) and also graduate diplomas for intending teachers, but all students who wish to qualify for teaching posts in LEA schools must undertake at least one year's further training at a college of education. Graduate status carries with it the eligibility for higher earning scales.

Music degrees proper can be taken as part of the programme of study at the Royal Academy of Music, the Royal College of Music, Trinity College of Music, London, Royal Northern College of Music, College of St Mark and St John (jointly with education diploma), Goldsmith's College, and under Council for National Academic Awards at Huddersfield Polytechnic, Colchester Technical College and School of Art, Hendon College of Technology, Dartington College of Arts, and Newton Park College of Higher Education.

It must be said that many who set out to become solo performers fail to realise that ambition and opt for teaching as a second choice. However, as instrumental teachers in schools they may have a much higher performance, and thus inspirational, standard than those who enter the teaching side of the profession as a first choice by way of university or college of education. A certain number become frustrated performers it is true; but most settle down to their different role with enthusiasm and effectiveness, succeeding in combining enough casual performing engagements as soloists or orchestral players to maintain their personal standards and their all-important links with the world of music-making.

The criticism of the colleges of music most frequently voiced by former students is that of lack of guidance about the profession as a whole, and about the attitudes of orchestras, concert societies, agents, and organisations like the BBC and the Arts Council. Similar criticisms are often made of poor career advice at universities. In both colleges and universities there is a career advice service, but however expert dons may be in their own specialist field, or college professors may be in teaching, say, the piano, career advice often seems to be out of touch with current professional life and irrelevant to the needs of the individual student at the crucial moment of planning the future. Students of orchestral instruments are more fortunate in this respect, as their professors are often playing members of well-known orchestras. Pianists and general musicians are the least well served. For all there is a lack of what might be called basic general advice about life in the profession.

It may be that the reduction in the number of students at the colleges again advocated in the Gulbenkian Report, together with adequate arrangements for direct financing will, if adopted, lead to students enjoying a fuller campus life and a greater degree of individual attention and tutoring.

Whatever reforms may be instituted, however, it is clear that in the nature of the music profession students must learn to make and maintain their own contacts with experienced practising musicians and to keep up to date with developments in the branch of music they wish to enter. The performers courses set up at Snape Maltings are admirable, and it is hoped that the policy of the National Opera Studio, with close connections with the main opera companies, will prove to be another important step in the right direction.

The main music colleges and schools of music and drama offering a full musical education are listed in Appendix 4.

UNIVERSITIES

IT IS A mistake—not confined to those who have no experience of study in any arts subject at university—to imagine that courses in music there provide some sort of gateway into the professional world or blueprint of career structure for graduates. On the whole, with certain differences of emphasis, all university degree courses have in common the academic discipline of the history of music and its structures, with special reference to harmony and counterpoint. But beyond that they offer a wide variety of specialisation, ranging from electronics in composition to practical technical electronics for the broadcasting and recording industries; from undergraduate instrumental skills suited to the needs of student composers, to organ music for scholars still closely linked to college chapels and the liturgies of the Established Church, with music of the sixteenth and seventeenth centuries rather than that of the twentieth. The variety is immense and constantly changing.

As in the academic disciplines of, say, mathematics or medicine, the best thing aspiring students can do is to study closely the specialisations offered by each of the universities and music departments, and above all to find out as much as possible about the people on the staff who run the departments and who teach there. For instance, due to the drive of Wilfrid Mellers, York University has collected on its staff a group of composers representing most of the current musical movements in the world; and although the individuals change from time to time, the group remains comprehensive. In addition there are the splendid facilities of the Lyons Music Centre, available for performances of every kind and for sophisticated technological experiment. Alun Hoddinott's influence has developed Cardiff along similar lines with excellent facilities for composers.

At Manchester there has long been a traditional link between the university and the Royal Northern College of Music in the form of a joint BA course, with emphasis on the need to learn an instrument thoroughly. At nearby Salford the speciality is the development of skills for the technical sides of mass reproduction in recording and broadcasting. Birmingham and Nottingham have a long history of distinguished professors and lecturers, and many fine stage performances of early operas and masques have been researched, edited and performed there.

Aberystwyth pioneered that splendid idea of having a residential string quartet or other instrumental ensemble, enabling the members to learn a wide repertoire and to gain invaluable performing experience, while at the same time inspiring the whole musical life of the university in many ways. Many have followed this lead, including Lancaster, Warwick, York, Edinburgh, Sussex, Keele and Liverpool. And, of course, Durham has for long been the main source of external as well as internal degrees, with many doctors of music of fame and high international standing to its credit.

The biggest problem, strangely enough, may arise for those who go up to Oxford or Cambridge, to the oldest and best established courses. So many people are misled by the glamour of the college names, their undoubted architectural beauty, the talented students they attract and the intellectual advantages they have over later foundations, that they embark upon degree courses unaware of the real aims and limitations of Oxford and Cambridge. Students there must be willing and able to work with the minimum of supervision and direction; they must know how to take advantage of a bewildering amount of musical activity in a purposeful as well as in an interesting way, in the absence of a focal centre such as they would find at other universities. They must develop also their own sense of professional standards and practicalities, and above all learn how to organise their own aims and activities. All this is fine for those with an organising flair, like the bright Cambridge group of the fifties who graduated from the Footlights' revues to performing versions of Cavalli operas at Glyndebourne, or more recently the Kings Singers with their neo-Swingle revivification of English part-songs. It is excellent also for those who hope to become music directors at schools, or cathedral organists. But some students who entered Cambridge or Oxford with high hopes have become frustrated through lack of adequate direction from their tutors and have ended up drifting around in a rather amateur way, getting nowhere. They may even give up music.

For those young musicians, however, who understand the nature of the courses and the way of life at Oxford and Cambridge, the opportunities and openings are simply wonderful. The mode of existence is still so interesting and romantic that it is small wonder that many young musicians find it hard to adjust to the realities of professional life in the world outside and choose jobs which will keep them within the academic orbit.

Many young graduates from all universities who possess a flair for organisation go on into arts administration, as do quite a number of classics and economics graduates, usually taking on various 'dogsbody' jobs in theatres, orchestras or agents' offices before applying for one of the Arts Council's sponsored courses in arts administration at the City University, London, (post-graduate diploma) or the Polytechnic of Central London (a variety of courses) or other places. All these courses involve very valuable 'secondments' to major professional organisations of every kind.

Wherever the student goes, to whatever university with whatever specialisation, it is very useful indeed to continue expert professional lessons in his or her main instrument (or voice). In most cases these will have to be extra-mural and paid for separately, but they are essential if the student is to maintain a link with the world of actual music-making. Another skill which should be acquired and practised so that it becomes second nature is keyboard facility. There is no need to aspire to concerto techniques or recital repertoire; it is sufficient to attain the degree of keyboard facility which will enable the student to be at home at the piano, with or without music and able to accompany anything simple by ear and anything more complicated by the shorthand method of playing the essentials—competent to play for class lessons and private pupils.

In addition to the undergraduate courses in music some universities offer postgraduate courses leading to a Dip.Ed. (Diploma in Education to teach music) which are available to graduates of music colleges and technical institutions as well as to university graduates. It is important for prospective students to obtain full details of qualifications required and facilities offered from the university of their choice, but the following universities offer a Dip.Ed. related to music teaching with a variety of special conditions:

Birmingham	Cambridge	Reading
Leeds	Hull	Durham
Manchester	Sheffield	London
Newcastle	York	Bangor
Aberystwyth	Southampton	Cardiff
Oxford		

See Appendix 5 for a full list of universities offering music as a degree subject.

TRAINING OF MUSIC TEACHERS FOR SCHOOLS

MUSIC TEACHERS IN schools have a wide variety of functions to fulfil, ranging from organising class-singing, giving instruction in musical appreciation and preparing students for 'O' and 'A' level examinations, to organising the work of visiting instrumental teachers (and perhaps teaching an instrument themselves), arranging school concerts and a host of other activities. In some schools they may be engaged solely in musical work; in others they may also teach general subjects.

The training for this work may start at a music college or at a college of education, but the requirements for it and the provision of training for future teachers is undergoing radical change, unlikely to be settled for a long time. Prospective candidates are, therefore, recommended to apply to their local education authority for up-to-date information.

Teacher training may also be undertaken at one of the polytechnics or institutes of higher education. Some of the former colleges have already been merged with polytechnics; one or two have merged with universities and others may follow suit; others have become institutes of higher education. All of them offer Diplomas of Higher Education or degrees of Bachelor of Education.

The polytechnics, of course, fulfil an important role in providing a variety of music courses at pre-college level; this was referred to earlier. Many also offer full courses in music and a wide range of useful specialist courses, such as that in organ building in Leamington Spa, the course for studio managers and electronic engineering (for radio, television and the recording industry) at Huddersfield and Surrey, not to mention the many courses which have brought so many distinguished musicians to help at Morley College, Southwark.

For a list of technical colleges offering music courses see Appendix 3.

COURSES IN ARTS ADMINISTRATION

UNTIL THE FORMATION of the Arts Council of Great Britain in 1944 the administration of the theatre and music worlds was mainly in the hands of the great actor and conductor managers; famous impresarios like Sir Henry Wood, Sir Thomas Beecham and Sir Malcolm Sargent, who promoted concerts, raised money from patrons, arranged parts and generally 'ran the show'.

The advent of subsidised theatre and permanent orchestras, with financial aid from the Arts Council of Great Britain, through grants-in-aid from central government, and the involvement of local authorities in the arts directly, and indirectly through regional arts associations, as well as sponsorship from industry and commerce, revealed a shortage of trained administrators able to run large and increasingly complex enterprises.

To meet the need for specialist-trained people the Arts Council of Great Britain set up a training department covering many aspects of the arts including administration. Full details of these and many other courses, including those which are partly sponsored by the Arts Council, and independent courses, can be obtained on application to:

THE TRAINING OFFICER at the ARTS COUNCIL OF GREAT BRITAIN, 105 Piccadilly, London W1V 0AU.

MAIN SPONSORED COURSES

CITY OF LONDON UNIVERSITY, St John Street, London EC1Y 4PB. Several courses are now run, two in association with the Arts Council of Great Britain. They are:

DIPLOMA IN ARTS ADMINISTRATION. This is a one-year post-graduate course for students over twenty-one with some experience in one or more artistic fields. The first two terms are devoted to the structure of the arts in Great Britain, with intensive courses in various aspects of management, principles and case studies. The third term is spent on secondment to an appropriate organisation—opera, orchestra, concert management or arts centre, and the production of a short thesis. There is throughout a tutorial system with visiting administrators from various arts organisations.

PRACTICAL COURSE. Students on this course undertake several different secondments, of varying durations, to arts organisations, with a concentrated six weeks of academic management study about mid-way through the course, which includes visits of speakers from important arts organisations.

Students may apply for either or both courses and they are helped in their choice by means of informal open meetings held at the Arts Council offices and attended by representatives of specialist departments, namely music, drama and art.

Bursaries are available (subject to various conditions) from:

SOCIAL SCIENCE RESEARCH COUNCIL (SSRC),
1 Temple Avenue, London EC4Y 0BD;

TRAINING OPPORTUNITIES SCHEME (TOPS),
through the candidates own Dept. of Employment office;

THE ARTS COUNCIL itself,
105 Piccadilly, London W1V 0AU.
(also the Scottish and Welsh offices where appropriate).

POLYTECHNIC OF CENTRAL LONDON,
35 Marylebone Road, London NW1 5LS,
also offers several courses in arts administration.

OTHER PROFESSIONAL TRAINING ORGANISATIONS

THE NATIONAL OPERA STUDIO has been formed as a result of the report of the working party set up by the Arts Council of Great Britain to enquire into the facilities for advanced opera training in Britain with special reference to the future of the London Opera Centre. The main recommendation was that many aspects of advanced student training were now being undertaken by the music colleges and the need for the future would be for experience more nearly connected to the professional opera companies. The National Opera Studio will concentrate on preparing young professional singers in special areas of the repertoire and in specific roles in close consultation with the opera companies, whose managing directors and general administrators form its board of directors. A very limited number of singers can be taken each year, about twelve plus three trainee repetiteurs, all nominated by the opera companies, colleges of music and leading singing teachers.

Full details and prospectus can be obtained from the Administrator at:

NATIONAL OPERA STUDIO,
1 Mermaid Court, Borough High Street, London SE1.

THE ROYAL MILITARY SCHOOL OF MUSIC, founded in 1857, is housed at Kneller Hall, Twickenham, and caters for two categories of musicians. Pupils enlisted in army bands may be sent on a one-year course on their principal instrument and on a stringed instrument or piano. Pupils who show talent and qualities of leadership may return later to Kneller Hall for a three-year course leading to a qualification as bandmaster. For this the student is given a thorough training on all band instruments, in choral and instrumental music, form, harmony, counterpoint, arranging and conducting. During the three-year course which leads to a Bandmaster's Certificate, attracting world-wide recognition, students are encouraged to study for and take the exams and diplomas of the Royal College of Music, the Royal Academy of Music or of the other music colleges.

THE ROYAL COLLEGE OF ORGANISTS in Kensington Gore, London administers external examinations only, offering qualifications of FRCO, ARCO and FRCO (CHM—Church Music). All examinations are taken in London twice yearly (CHM annually). Master classes and lectures in various centres are the only other activities.

THE ROYAL SCHOOL OF CHURCH MUSIC was founded in 1927 to encourage the study and practice of music and of speech for church services. It offers a wide variety of short courses at Addington Palace, Croydon and elsewhere, and it gives practical help to affiliated churches, colleges and schools throughout the world. Membership is open to organisations and to individuals of all Christian denominations.

BRIDGES INTO THE PROFESSION

FOR SOME YOUNG people the transition from being a student to life as a professional presents no problems. Many young instrumentalists gain quite a lot of experience with professional orchestras as deputies and extras during their college days. Some wind players are picked out as potential recruits by leading principals,

Kneller Hall trumpeters of the Royal Military School of Music.

managers and conductors, fine string players are in constant demand all over the world. The danger for them is that of getting swept up in the hurly-burly of orchestral life without having the time or the opportunity to continue to develop their individual skills by regular master lessons and coaching. They must avoid getting into a situation which, however exciting it may be at first, can easily become a rut after a few years.

But for many there is a quite different hazard, that of putting off the day of full commitment and drifting along in a state of perpetual studentship. For soloists, conductors and composers a long apprenticeship is inevitable, but aspirants in these categories would do well to undertake some work, however humble or menial, to give them a taste for work and to enable them to acquaint themselves with musical activity of all kinds and at all levels.

Among the most successful conductors of the day, those in the German and Italian schools learn their trade in opera houses doing a wide range of coaching and repetiteur work, going from *vierter Kapellmeister* through all the stages of minor provincial and principal theatres to the position of *erster Kapellmeister* and principal conductor of one of the great symphony orchestras. Böhm, Karajan, Klemperer, Horenstein, Szell and countless others all rose to international pre-eminence in this way.

Toscanini, Barbirolli, Giulini and Colin Davies are examples of those con-ductors whose apprenticeships were as orchestral players. Bernstein and Previn are outstanding examples of pianists who succeeded by superb general musi-cianship, writing music for and performing in the world of light music as naturally and brilliantly as they handle the standard repertoire and modern serious music.

Among composers, too, one need not look far to see that experience as a performer (Britten), as a teacher (Tippett) and as an orchestral player (Malcolm Arnold) provides both 'bread and butter' and invaluable personal experience for composition.

For pianists the way ahead is more difficult—the opportunities for securing prestigious concerto and recital engagements are few. But in accepting a variety of work—accompanying singers and instrumentalists, playing for choral societies' rehearsals and amateur opera companies—their keyboard facility will be devel-oped and their knowledge of general musical repertoire extended, bringing them into contact with working musicians and providing them with a means of earning a livelihood. John Pritchard is a marvellous example of a musician with the highest standards, amazing instinctive insight into interpretation, combined with wide practical ability, derived from working with every level of music-making, professional and amateur, and the assiduous pursuit of first-hand experience by attending rehearsals of top-class international soloists, conductors, orchestras and opera companies.

So the first bridge into the profession is self-help. Go on studying always; but do some practical work as well. Don't blame circumstances if the way is difficult; make your own opportunities.

SCHOLARSHIP FUNDS

The second bridge is provided by the large number of privately endowed trusts and scholarships offering a wide variety of grants to talented young musicians in different fields. There are grants for study abroad, coaching for auditions, commissioning fees for composers, recitals for launching young artists, purchase of instruments and many other needs. A list is compiled each year by the Arts Council of Great Britain, setting out the general aims and conditions of all the scholarships and the names and addresses of the officials to write to. It is freely available on request. There are in addition one or two major trusts, such as the Ralph Vaughan Williams Trust, which avoid publicity but give substantial help to hundreds of musicians every year for a very wide range of projects strongly directed towards crossing the bridge between studenthood and professional life.

There are also innumerable other private trusts ranging from the City Livery Companies to private firms and individuals from whom grants may be obtained, usually on the basis of personal recommendation. Many are listed in a booklet issued by the NUS Educational Trusts. However the Arts Council list, though it omits these intentionally, is sufficiently comprehensive to constitute essential reading. The following are just a few examples of the more important scholarships and bursaries available:

General: COUNTESS OF MUNSTER MUSICAL TRUST,
The Secretary, Wormley Hill, Godalming, Surrey GU8 5SQ;

MARTIN MUSICAL SCHOLARSHIP FUND,
The Secretary, 12 de Walden Court, 85 New Cavendish Street, London W1;

RALPH VAUGHAN WILLIAMS TRUST,
16 Ogle Street, London W1;

Composers: ARTS COUNCIL OF GREAT BRITAIN bursaries and commission fees, Mendelssohn Scholarship, The Secretary, 14 Bedford Square, London WC1B 3JG;

THE HINRICHSEN FOUNDATION,
c/o Royal Philharmonic Society, 124 Wigmore Street, London W1;

Singers: KATHLEEN FERRIER MEMORIAL SCHOLARSHIP FUND,
RPS, 124 Wigmore Street, London W1;

General: BRITISH COUNCIL, on behalf of the Governments of Austria, Belgium, Bulgaria, Czechoslovakia, Denmark, Finland, France, Germany, Greece, Hungary, Italy, Japan, Netherlands, Poland, Romania, USSR, Sweden,
Higher Education Department, 10 Spring Gardens, London SW1A 2BN;

Orchestral instruments: SHELL-LONDON SYMPHONY ORCHESTRA SCHOLARSHIP,
Administrator, Regent Arcade House, 19/25 Argyll Street, London W1.

The competition for grants from any of these scholarship funds and trusts is very keen and applicants are advised to find out exactly what is offered and what standards are expected to ensure that their applications will be considered.

But for most students, those who want to study abroad, in Russia or America for example, or do the singer's audition circuit in Germany or Italy, attend master classes, undertake research projects in new or neglected music, get practical experience in new techniques of composition or of teaching; or go on after graduating from university to an intensive performer's course for a year, or for those who need an instrument more suitable for professional use than their student one; for these and many other aims the scholarship, trust and bursary funds can and do provide a valuable bridge into the profession.

INTERNATIONAL COMPETITIONS

At this stage many young aspirant virtuosi will want to try their luck in one of the many international competitions that have become so important a part of the post-war music scene. A comprehensive revised list of major competitions in Britain and abroad appears in the *British Music Yearbook*. Amongst the most famous are our own Leeds International Pianoforte Competition; the International Tchaikovsky Competition (piano, violin, cello and voice) in Moscow; the

The first three winners of the Leeds International Pianoforte Competition: Michael Roll (left), Radu Lupu (centre), Rafael Orozco (right), together after the 1972 Final won by Murray Perahia.

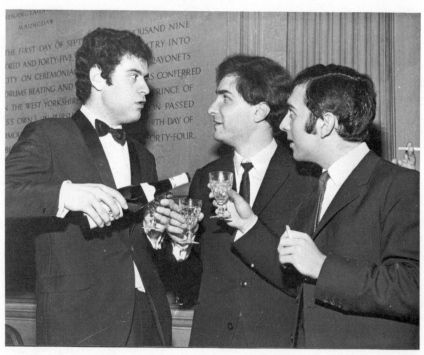

comprehensive Bavarian State Radio Competitions in Munich; the Carl Flesch Violin Prize in London and hundreds of others for composers, conductors, singers and every type of instrumentalist.

There are many who oppose the whole competition principle as being detrimental to the best interests of young musicians. Certainly there are dangers, especially those of exposing a subtle talent in an atmosphere favouring more robust gifts and of risking an already growing reputation by premature comparisons with others. An even greater hazard is perhaps that of winning and being offered engagements on a scale beyond the student's repertoire capabilities at that time; or worse, perhaps, of winning and imagining that the hard work is over—it isn't, it's just beginning!

But the critics overlook the fact that on the whole, juries have a curious instinct for picking the right ones, a fact to which Zubin Mehta, Ashkenazy, Pinchas Zukerman, Claudio Abbado, Pollini, and others too numerous to list, bear eloquent testimony. If they are entered in the right spirit, competitions provide an opportunity of comparing oneself with the best of one's generation in the world and of being heard by many impresarios and managers as well as by famous musicians. At most of them a wonderful spirit prevails among the competitors—one happy memory is that of Gwyneth Jones and her rival sopranos lending each other jewellery and helping each other with dresses and so on in one competition; another is of the extraordinary support all the Leeds winners (and non-winners) give each other at their various London appearances in subsequent years.

It is advisable to study all the aspects of a competition before entering for it; get to know all you can of its standards and any bias it may have towards this or that approach to technique or interpretation. Make sure it's really for you. Also, by the time you've paid entrance fees, travel and subsistence it can work out very expensive; so make your approach to any trust or benefactors as early as possible.

However, it cannot be stressed too strongly or too frequently, that the most important bridge into the profession of music is the one which must be constructed by the aspirants themselves. It must be assumed at this stage that each young musician has genuine talent, natural aptitude, a good constitution mentally and physically, has had a proper grounding technically in all the skills required for the branch of music to be entered into and has that affection for music and instinctive compulsion to practice it which are the essential foundations on which to build a career.

With this equipment he or she is now ready for the first steps in the world of professional music. It will have cost parents and education authorities a total capital outlay of anything up to £12,000 or £15,000 to get a student this far, that is for ten to twelve years of lessons during school years; three or four years at college, plus a modest instrument. So what sort of a career can be made in professional life?

SECTION III

The Life of the Professional Musician

BEFORE CONSIDERING in detail the many branches of the music profession, and outlining their various requirements and rewards, there are certain fundamental characteristics which are relevant to them all.

The first thing to remember is that you are addressing an audience, as a performer, composer, teacher, musicologist, administrator or critic. You hope to serve the art of music and in its service to earn your living, but it is vital to be constantly aware of the need to address your audience—of concert goers, students, readers of papers and journals or listeners to broadcasts.

The second concerns the acquisition of some elementary business skills. Do try to write clear concise letters; learn to keep simple accounts using a day journal and to type if you can (you really can teach yourself to type quite quickly). It is important to learn about insurance, taxation and VAT. It may be years before success permits you to leave such matters to others, agents or managers or secretaries, and even then it's very useful to be able to check things yourself.

The third is the most important of all—study the market. Market research is as vital to the musician as it is to the salesman of any other commodity or service. Study the market thoroughly and in detail. Learn as much as you can about any organisations you want to get into—exactly what they do; in what categories of repertoire and styles; at what levels; what they pay; the names of leading officials, not forgetting their titles and honours, and as much about them as possible. This applies to every type of job from membership of an orchestra to solo recitals in music clubs; from approaching conductors for concerto dates to asking for broadcasts; from any sort of administration job to peripatetic teaching for a local education authority.

Except in the most unusual circumstances you are entering a buyer's market; you have to convince someone that they want you. So study the market and keep up to date.

OPPOSITE

André Previn and the London Symphony Orchestra at the Proms.

Some books and journals for essential references are listed in Appendix 16.

The major National Organisations concerned with music and their addresses are given in Appendix 7.

PROFESSIONAL ORCHESTRAS

IT WILL BE most practical to deal with professional orchestras first because they provide the major source of employment in the performing world; few soloists, apart from pianists and singers (and not many of those) can make a living as soloists alone. Most instrumentalists are glad to have a basis for their work in some form of orchestral playing or, of course, in teaching—or a combination of both.

Furthermore, the idiosyncratic manner of the orchestras' establishment in Britain gives a clue to the marked differences in overall musical organisation between this country and say, Germany, upon whose musical traditions we have drawn so heavily in all other respects.

It is not generally known that until the formation of the BBC Symphony Orchestra in 1930 there had been no full-time, salaried, symphony orchestra in Britain. The Hallé Orchestra in Manchester, founded in 1859 and the even earlier Royal Liverpool Philharmonic, founded in 1840, and similar orchestras had long been on the musical scene, but they were seasonal orchestras formed to play some twelve to sixteen subscription concerts annually in their home towns and, in the case of the Hallé, repeating some of the concerts in other big cities like Bradford and Sheffield. They also came together for the great choral festivals like those at Norwich, Leeds, York, Birmingham and the Three Choirs. But at best it was a part-time, ad hoc, fee-earning, rather than salaried occupation. It gave the members a status which enabled them to establish good teaching connections, engagements for solo recitals and occasional work in the theatre. Right up to the last war most of the players were engaged for the summer season at one of the holiday resorts: Brighton, Harrogate, Scarborough, Torquay, Bexhill, and others including Llandudno, where the late Sir Malcolm Sargent conducted some fifty concerts, each with a different programme every summer season. Conductors like Sargent learned their trade thoroughly in this way, arranging many large orchestral works for bands of about forty or fifty and putting on the concerts with at best a play-through rehearsal, often with none at all, so that conductors and players alike had to know their music thoroughly.

If orchestral music in the provinces was dependent upon the local philharmonic and concert societies, and built upon the emergence of the great choral festivals (reflecting in turn the religious emancipation of the late eighteenth and early nineteenth centuries) and the summer seasons, in London the orchestras provided music for another kind of singing, that of the theatre and the pleasure gardens. Under the Licensing Act of 1737 and right up to 1840 all theatres had to show only presentations and plays with music—ironically Covent Garden and Drury Lane were the only theatres exempted under Royal Patent from this restriction, together with the Haymarket for summer seasons. Sadlers Wells theatre made many attempts to get exemption too, but failed every time.

Thus there developed in the eighteenth and early nineteenth centuries the great tradition of singing actors who, by the way, were frequently their own composers, script-writers, producers, theatre managers and impresarios; a brilliant breed stretching from Dibden, Grimaldi and Garrick to Beerbohm Tree, Martin Harvey and Donald Wolfit in recent times. Their achievements were matched only by their phenomenal stamina. Every theatre had its own orchestra and for the players the steady money—the bread and butter—was in the pit; the artistic cake was in the occasional concert hall appearance. The attitudes thus established and crystallised remain to this day a powerful if slightly obscured factor in the London orchestral situation, where, as will shortly be described in more detail, there are still no salaried orchestras outside the BBC and the opera houses.

Orchestras were assembled by impresarios for a 'season' of concerts, often connected with the visits of distinguished composers like Hadyn, Mozart or Mendelssohn. These impresarios knew all the best players—those who were adept as quick readers from the experience and nature of their work in the theatre pit and the pleasure gardens. The stimulus of working with a great musician in a different type and category of music resulted in a fresh, alert manner of playing which gained for the London bands an international reputation. From this situation developed the deputy system—deputies such as pupils and friends took over in the theatre from any regular players engaged for the concerts. Boulez tells a lovely story about Paris in the present day—the principal double bass couldn't get a deputy and in despair sent along as deputy the concierge from his flats. It so happened that all the basses were deputies that evening, and all concierges. 'But', adds Boulez, 'it didn't matter because the conductor, he was a concierge too!'

Similar situations persist in London to this day. For theatre pit read recording, film, television and advertising studios. The players in the four major independent orchestras and many well-known chamber orchestras and smaller ensembles are fee-earning, not salaried, and they derive much of their income from these lucrative fringe activities, public concerts remaining something of an artistic but comparatively unremunerative luxury. The deputy system, though better controlled by the parent orchestras nowadays, still persists.

However, no one who was involved in orchestral music in London or the provinces before the war could have anticipated the wonderful strides which have been made in so short a time in developing splendid standards of orchestral playing all over the country and establishing generally a much more stable and well-organised orchestral profession.

Good players are in demand here at home and all over Europe, East and West, as well as in America, Russia, Japan, Australia, Canada and Africa, and a young instrumentalist can make a good and interesting career in the orchestral world.

The organisation of orchestras can be conveniently separated under three main headings, each with several sub-categories. It should be understood that players are able to move around quite freely between one type of orchestra and another, making a progression in rank and standing wholly to the benefit of themselves and the profession. Conductors and managers, understandably disappointed at the loss of some young player trained in their orchestra, sometimes make rather too much of what is and should be a normal state of affairs. Unlike footballers, neither the club nor the player benefits by transfer fees! It must also be remembered that conditions of too great stability can become dangerous in the arts and often lead to stagnation. One of the counter-proverbs runs: 'Still waters are stagnant and frequently stink.'

The three main categories of professional orchestras in Britain are:

1. salaried orchestras with continuing contracts;

2. orchestras engaged on a regular fee-paying, work-session basis;
3. orchestras engaging players on an occasional fee-paying, work-session basis.

It is essential for professional musicians, in all categories of orchestra to be members of the Musicians Union. The main organisation co-ordinating salaries, fees and conditions of work with the Musicians Union on behalf of the various categories of orchestras is the Association of British Orchestras, but the BBC and the opera and theatre managements negotiate directly with the union in respect of their employment contracts.

1. SALARIED ORCHESTRAS

(a) REGIONAL ORCHESTRAS

There are now five full-time symphony orchestras and three smaller orchestras, all on a salaried basis of employment.

The five symphony orchestras:

>THE BOURNEMOUTH SYMPHONY ORCHESTRA;
>
>THE CITY OF BIRMINGHAM SYMPHONY ORCHESTRA;
>
>THE HALLÉ ORCHESTRA (MANCHESTER);
>
>THE ROYAL LIVERPOOL PHILHARMONIC ORCHESTRA;
>
>THE SCOTTISH NATIONAL ORCHESTRA (GLASGOW).

The three other orchestras:

>THE BOURNEMOUTH SINFONIETTA;
>
>THE NORTHERN SINFONIA (NEWCASTLE);
>
>THE ULSTER ORCHESTRA (BELFAST).

Employment with these orchestras is on the basis of the standard contract agreed with the Musicians Union through the Association of British Orchestras.

The contract regulates the number of working hours per day, per week and per four-week period which may be scheduled by the managements within a basic five-day week. It sets out the method of calculating overtime for extra hours worked or types of work, such as recording, for which there is a higher payment rate; it fixes travel and subsistence rates for work out of town and all other matters, such as holidays, appointments and dismissals, salaries, rates of various grades of player from principal to rank and file strings, and pension rights.

Although a great deal has been done to effect security and stability of employment for members of these orchestras, the salaries are still not high. If one takes into account the costs of training; of buying and maintaining instruments; of providing tail-suits, dinner jackets and dark suits for public concerts; of spending a considerable amount of time travelling and waiting between rehearsals and concerts, not to mention the high degree of skill required, the 1977 salaries of between £3,500 p.a. for rank and file players and £4,000 p.a. for principals do not represent riches.

On the other hand the players usually have time to undertake some teaching of private pupils, chamber music, solo work and even a certain amount of work in their free time for other orchestras as deputies and extras when large-scale works like Berlioz' *Grande Messe*, Mahler's Eighth Symphony or Schönberg's *Gurrelieder* are being performed. But the chief virtues of life in one of these regional orchestras lie in the experience gained from the large repertoire undertaken, the development of the corporate spirit, the close relationship formed with the musical public (in cities like Liverpool or Manchester members of the orchestra are known individually by large sections of the public) and the security of tenure.

The artistic policy and repertoire of a regional orchestra is harnessed to provide attractive programmes of wide-ranging styles as a public service. And so the work undertaken by a regional orchestra falls into the following pattern, with the principal conductor, guest conductors and, nowadays, a wonderful range of soloists from the famous internationals to the young emerging stars.

Home Town

Main series of fortnightly subscription concerts; weekly popular concerts; series for industry, commerce and business; choral, Christmas and seasonal concerts; proms and summer series.

Other Towns

Programmes made up of works played in the various home town series with occasional visits to London's Royal Festival Hall, the BBC Proms, or festivals such as Edinburgh with special programmes.

Touring Abroad

Occasional tours abroad usually arranged with the help of the British Council.

BBC

Occasional live relays from public concerts, or pre-recording for later transmission—mainly on radio, but also on TV for special occasions such as the Leeds International Pianoforte Competition.

Commercial Recording

For the regional orchestras this is mostly connected with the relationship between conductors and recording companies—Sir Malcolm Sargent and the Liverpool Philharmonic and Sir John Barbirolli and the Hallé, both with the companies now amalgamated as EMI, are two such past associations. The records they made are still on the market. At present Sir Alexander Gibson and the Scottish National, James Loughran and the Hallé, Sir Charles Groves and the Royal Liverpool, Louis Fremaux and the Birmingham and Paavo Berglund and the Bournemouth all make records reflecting their own special tastes and expertise.

The employment of these regional orchestras is the responsibility of independent committees of management, comprising in each place representatives of the musical public, nominees of the local authority, some form of player representation, with an Arts Council of Great Britain assessor. The principal conductor and the general manager are also appointed by these management committees and they in turn are responsible for advising the committees on all artistic and technical matters and for carrying out in detail the policies decided upon.

In 1977 the annual expenditure of such orchestras ranged from about £500,000 to £1,000,000 for the five symphony orchestras and from £250,000 to £400,000 for the three smaller orchestras. The symphony orchestras derive their income in roughly three equal parts—from earned income (ticket sales and hired engagement fees), the Arts Council of Great Britain, and local authorities. The proportions of earned income are much lower for the three smaller orchestras as their work is mostly in the thinly populated and rural areas of the West Country, Northern Ireland, Cumbria and the country areas of North Yorkshire, Durham and Northumberland.

(b) BBC ORCHESTRAS

The main differences between the BBC staff orchestras and the regional orchestras are the method of financing and the nature of the work.

The BBC staff orchestras are wholly financed out of licence fees. From time to time they receive payments for playing at certain public concerts or from sale of tickets at the London proms, but these earnings only cover the additional cost of travel, subsistence, special soloists or anything else arising from playing outside their studios. Such income does not go towards the cost of salaries or similar normal costs of maintenance.

The purpose of the orchestras is, of course, to provide a broadcasting service, regionally and nationally, and all performances in the studio or in public must be broadcast. This involves the staff orchestras in playing a very large repertoire indeed to avoid 'repeats'. The artistic policy is influenced by the requirements of network planners.

The level of salaries paid to members of BBC staff orchestras is very similar to that of those received by the salaried regional orchestras, though the BBC Symphony Orchestra in London has special rates. The conditions of service, holidays, working hours, pensions and sickness benefits are also comparable, but security of tenure extends beyond any individual orchestra to the whole corpus of BBC orchestral employment.

Some musicians like the pattern of life offered which frequently gives a working day of 9.30–5.30 leaving evenings free (unlike other orchestras); some feel keenly the lack of audience and the troglodyte atmosphere of the studios, although in recent years arrangements have been made with the regional orchestras to permit more concerts in public. There is no doubt, however, that the discipline of high individual playing standards demanded by the microphone and the value of learning so large a repertoire in a short time make a period spent in a BBC staff orchestra a most valuable experience, even for those players who prefer more public performance.

The BBC staff orchestras are:

London:	BBC SYMPHONY ORCHESTRA
	BBC CONCERT ORCHESTRA
Manchester:	BBC NORTHERN SYMPHONY ORCHESTRA
Glasgow:	BBC SCOTTISH SYMPHONY ORCHESTRA
Cardiff:	BBC WELSH ORCHESTRA—augmented by arrangement with the Welsh Arts Council and performing an agreed number of public concerts.
Belfast:	BBC NORTH OF IRELAND ORCHESTRA

(c) OPERA AND BALLET ORCHESTRAS

For members of the orchestras of the two main London opera companies working life in the theatre pit is even more anonymous than that of the BBC orchestras in the studios. The Royal Opera House and the Coliseum maintain large orchestras of some 135 players working a rota system. The productions of opera and ballet changes nightly in true repertory for seasons of so many weeks so that there is much repetition for the orchestra. They work a system of seven three-hour shifts per week for either rehearsals or performances in return for their basic salaries. There are special rates for touring and adjustments for more highly-paid work such as recording.

Glyndebourne Festival Opera has an arrangement with the London Philharmonic Orchestra to provide the opera orchestra for the season (May–August) on terms specially related to the nature of the orchestra's own conditions of membership and work. For the Glyndebourne Touring Opera usually one or other of the smaller orchestras is engaged for the duration of the tours, providing a welcome income for the orchestra management and a change in routine for the players (delighting some and angering others!).

The Welsh National Opera has formed its own salaried orchestra to play for its opera seasons in Cardiff, Birmingham and elsewhere and to play concerts in public during the closed seasons—it is called the Welsh Philharmonia.

In Scotland the system works the other way round. Having started with the Scottish National Orchestra for its occasional opera seasons, Scottish Opera in its splendid new theatre home uses the Scottish Baroque Orchestra for its opera productions, paying them on a negotiated basis. The orchestra, which includes inter alia, some fine teachers from the Royal Scottish Academy of Music also plays concerts in different parts of Scotland. The rates for work in the opera pit are comparable with those in the salaried regional and BBC orchestras.

2. ORCHESTRAS ENGAGED ON A REGULAR, FEE-PAYING, WORK-SESSION BASIS

These are primarily the four independent self-governing London orchestras—in order of foundation:

THE LONDON SYMPHONY ORCHESTRA (1904);

THE LONDON PHILHARMONIC ORCHESTRA (1932);

THE ROYAL PHILHARMONIC ORCHESTRA (1945);

THE NEW PHILHARMONIA ORCHESTRA (1964)—reverting in 1977 to its original title of PHILHARMONIA ORCHESTRA (1943).

From the outset the LSO was formed by orchestral players themselves as a self-governing body to promote their own series of twelve to sixteen public concerts at the old Queens Hall with leading world conductors, and to be available for hire to other concert and choral societies, festivals and impresarios. The orchestra undertook some recording work and made such famous discs as *The Planets* under Holst, the Elgar Violin Concerto with the young Menuhin, the two Symphonies and *Falstaff* all under Elgar himself. They are still in the catalogue and are still greatly in demand.

All this work as an orchestra was fitted in between the other regular jobs of the individual members with the inevitable deputy system developing and causing conductors much frustration over fluctuating standards. At the worst a conductor might find himself with a substantial number of different players at each rehearsal, and at the performance with some players who had not been to any rehearsal at all. The leading member–directors of the LSO were also concerned and many purges and changes occurred in attempts to regulate the position.

Two of the other three orchestras were formed by Sir Thomas Beecham who wanted more control over the orchestras into which he poured so much of his own private wealth—before the family pharmaceutical business became a public company and his drawings were restricted to an allowance. First he formed the London Philharmonic and then, after the upheavals of the war years, the Royal Philharmonic, to the fury of Walter Legge who had expected Beecham to join him in the formation of the Philharmonia. Both calculated that they could capture the cream of the orchestral players demobbed from their various types of war service, by offering attractive work with the best conductors in the world, plenty of recording work and plenty of time to pursue their own individual ambitions of solo work and chamber music. Both men succeeded to a remarkable degree, temporarily at the expense of the BBC Symphony Orchestra and the LSO and LPO. The latter had become a salaried contract orchestra, but by the early 1950s their failure to be adopted as the House Orchestra of the new Royal Festival Hall, the inability of the Arts Council of Great Britain to provide a subsidy big enough to cover their inevitable operating deficit and the failure of the LCC to contribute on the scale undertaken by Liverpool and Birmingham, for instance, for their orchestras, brought them to financial collapse and caused them to revert to a self-governing status. Indeed it was their ownership of the freehold of a house in Welbeck Street, bought at rock bottom years earlier and by now immensely valuable, which enabled them to restart as a co-operative again.

The Royal Philharmonic was faced with a similar situation in 1963 with Beecham's withdrawal; and in 1964 when Walter Legge decided he could no longer maintain the Philharmonia at the standard he had aimed at and achieved for so long, he 'disbanded' the orchestra. The RPO had a desperate financial struggle to survive, meeting also with 'speed the poor traveller' death wishes in some official circles. The Philharmonia had an unpleasant wrangle over the title and several legal battles before the title New Philharmonia was agreed upon, but they were fortunate in retaining the loyalty of their great conductor Otto Klemperer and many other leading conductors, and with them obtained a stream of recordings with many companies as well as with EMI to whom they had previously been on exclusive contract.

There was in those days the added complication for all four independent orchestras that they could not receive direct subsidies from the Arts Council because of their constitutional status as self-governing and self-interested bodies. In an attempt to bring better order into the London scene Lord Goodman (then Mr Arnold Goodman) was commissioned to report on the situation. His recommendations, including the setting-up of an independent body—the London Orchestral Concerts Board (LOCB)—through which subsidies from the Arts Council and the GLC could be channelled to the four orchestras (and other organisations) represented a masterly example of British compromise, since the LOCB is made up solely of Arts Council and GLC representatives.

Under the LOCB scheme the four London orchestras are allocated some thirty dates each in the Royal Festival Hall and for these and perhaps ten more at the Fairfield Hall, Croydon, the Royal Albert Hall and and several other London venues, a total of forty own promotions in all, they receive a guarantee of some £2,000 per concert with added grants for administration costs, holiday, personal pension and sickness payments. There are additional guarantees for performances of new music.

In return the orchestras agree to a set of 'Marquis of Queensbury rules' principally governing avoidance of clashes of repertoire in the Royal Festival Hall and the enforcement of attendance rules for their own players. It is by no means a perfect system; in some respects it maintains the *status quo* of a situation arrived at largely through the arbitrary whim of conductors and impresarios of a different era.

But in some mysterious way the four do maintain their individual identities and styles of playing inherited from the nature and the personalities of their original establishment, despite the many changes of personnel and conductors they have undergone over the years. Each in its own way is unmistakable and each tends to attract the appropriate type of players as recruits. And they do provide London with a service of fine concerts with the world's leading conductors and soloists.

It should not be thought that the forty concerts each, for which subsidy is received from the LOCB, together with the hundred or so rehearsals that go with them, represent the total work-load. They are just the beginning, the basis upon which all their other work is obtained. In a recent year the London Symphony Orchestra worked the following schedule:

Own Concert promotions	39
Television series	30
Recording sessions	118
Hired concerts outside London including Edinburgh and other festivals	26
Tours abroad, USA, Japan Europe etc.	57

	270
Rehearsals total	236

This gives a total of 506 working sessions in the year (the totals of the other three London Orchestras in the same year were London Philharmonic 528, Royal Philharmonic 563, New Philharmonia 424. All members of these orchestras are bound to do eighty per cent of work offered by their own orchestra; in addition to which many carry out a busy schedule of commercial work, solo and ensemble engagements, and teaching. Young aspirants to London orchestral life face an arduous and exacting life style in return for an income about one and a half times that of the salaried orchestras described earlier.

These four listed in Section 2 have been described in some detail as, together with the BBC Symphony Orchestra and the orchestras of the Royal Opera House and the English National Opera, they form the main structure within which continuous orchestral employment in London exists.

There are, however, many other orchestras of varying sizes which also present their own series of concerts in London and elsewhere, and which offer their members a varying degree of regular if not continuous employment. Each has its own style, repertoire and following, and each has a nucleus of regular players drawn from the numerous chamber ensembles, soloists and freelance pool; partly also from the ranks of one or other of the larger regular orchestras.

These smaller specialist orchestras have become very popular in recent years with the upsurge of interest in early music, the baroque period and contemporary music. The English Chamber Orchestra, Academy of St Martin in the Fields, London Mozart Players, London Sinfonietta and others demand a high standard of playing and offer in return much broadcasting on radio and television, commercial recordings, tours abroad and engagements at the various festivals in Britain in addition to their own concerts. The fees paid (*ad hoc* by the engagement) are often at a slightly higher rate than those paid by the bigger orchestras. The repertoire is wide-ranging and very interesting.

A glance at the concert advertisement columns of the weekend newspapers will reveal a large number of miscellaneous really *ad hoc* orchestras which give occasional concerts and get occasional engagements. They are mostly got together from the freelance pool by various conductors for their own concerts and do not often achieve any greater identity or continuity of existence than that. Again standard fees are paid by the work session.

Finally many musicians start their careers, and many also end their playing days, in the widespread activity known as 'professional stiffening'. Throughout the country there are hundreds and hundreds of music societies presenting four or more choral or orchestral concerts each season. Most of them belong to the National Federation of Music Societies which uses a block grant from the Arts Council to subsidise the professional soloists and orchestral players required for their concerts. Sometimes a whole orchestra is engaged; often a few principal players are booked to 'stiffen' the local orchestra of teachers and amateurs. But young inexperienced players may encounter some hair-raising experiences: programmes consisting of less familiar choral works such as *These things shall be* (Ireland) or *Belshazzar's Feast* (Walton) or *A Child of our Time* (Tippett) on one three-hour rehearsal with conductors whose enthusiasm outruns their skill! On such occasions all depends on a firm experienced leader and good section principals to hold the work together.

The fees for this work are at the lowest rate agreed by the Union but it provides a useful source of income and social contacts for the numerous orchestral players who are willing to accept the work.

Whatever type of orchestra young players go into there are several general points to be borne in mind that will make life easier for them, and for their more experienced colleagues.

Join the Musicians Union and make sure your payments are kept up to date. Don't be misled by the cynical attitude manifested by some players; despite all appearances they do really care about standards and music itself—much of the blasé manner is put on to protect their real inner feelings and anxieties. Be a good partner and try to avoid mannerisms and habits which irritate the person with whom you are sharing a desk.

Do have your own pencil, rubber, rosin, mutes, spare strings and all the other bits and pieces you are sure to need.

However brilliantly you played at audition, no matter what solo dates you have coming up, don't practise concertos in the bandroom unless you want to become the most unpopular member of the orchestra.

If you haven't played a work before, even a repertoire piece, don't be ashamed to have a look at the part; you may save yourself from making a domino at rehearsal or performance and feeling an even bigger fool.

Do try to have occasional good coaching lessons; keep up your standard and enthusiasm for the sake of your own self-esteem as well as for the sake of the music.

A list of the main professional orchestras is given in Appendix 10.

SOLOISTS

A CAREER AS a soloist, although perhaps not so inevitably the ultimate aim as is popularly supposed, is nevertheless a general and very natural ambition among aspiring musicians. Indeed it may be said that all musicians, in every branch of the profession, should undertake some form of solo performance, at whatever level is appropriate throughout their careers as orchestral players, conductors, composers or teachers—and even administrators, musicologists and broadcasters too, if possible. It helps them to keep in touch with the sensations and feelings of performance and with the need for maintaining personal standards.

But a career just as a soloist makes demands that few can meet artistically, temperamentally or financially. At the very top there are a few stars in the fullest sense of the word, a mere handful able to command full houses everywhere in the world, sought after by all the great conductors, orchestras, festivals and concert societies. They have to have exceptional musical talent allied to many other personality factors, such as extra musical affection, mesmeric power, panache, even notoriety and unpredictability or the sort of apparent helplessness that still has a special appeal to some ladies. For these special stars fees are very high—up in the thousands for one performance; but the expenses are correspondingly high, with fees for agents, managers, air travel, cars, hotels, and taxation both at home and abroad swallowing up a large portion of the earnings. The duration of artistic life at this level may be limited and so may the number of organisations that can pay these top-bracket fees. Rubinstein once remarked that there is the additional hazard of never being able to play below one's very best without attracting unduly severe criticism.

If life in this very restricted 'premier league' is exacting, it is not much less so for the much larger first and second divisions, so to speak, of the soloists league. The fees for most international artists range from the middle to upper hundreds, with a few, especially opera singers, going something beyond the thousand mark, again less agency and management fees, taxes and expenses. There are more opportunities in the sense of there being many more organisations for whom fees of this level are the norm; but correspondingly there is much greater competition with the hundreds of other established pianists, violinists and singers in this category and with a constant stream of fine young players coming up from every new generation.

For all these full-time soloists the same basic requirements prevail. They must be totally dedicated, willing to forfeit many of the normal comforts of home and family life—travelling endlessly and living out of suitcases, moving in an artificial atmosphere, practising ceaselessly—and above all appear to be enjoying it all, as befits the star attraction of each concert. The letters of the great pianist Busoni, written to his wife while he was on tour in America, give a vivid description of the rigours of a soloist's life; so does Win Ferrier's biography of her famous sister Kathleen; the mode of travel changes, but the basic experience remains the same. Peter Pears remarked recently that the difference between 'then' and 'now' was merely that, whereas in the 'fifties he and Janet Baker and Heather Harper might meet at midnight at Crewe Station going from one *Messiah* at Hanley to another at Huddersfield, in the 'seventies they still meet at midnight awaiting connections at Tokyo, Moscow, Berlin or New York airports; one needs a strong constitution as well as musical skills.

Despite the rigours, the artistic rewards of a soloist's life are immense, which is why musicians remain attracted to it and why there is no shortage of contenders seeking promotion from the lower divisions and part-time work in the solo field, where the fees are smaller and the engagements more irregular. There is no set formula for promotion into the upper divisions. It may come through success in a competition; it may come through audition or being recommended by a teacher or a known soloist. All soloists have to endure the audition ordeal throughout their lives, both the direct audition and the more subtle forms, like knowing one is being listened to by 'scouts' during performance, or being summoned by one of the great conductors to sing a part for him with a view to inclusion in his next 'Mahler 4' or *Figaro*, for instance. Dr Klemperer had a very effective way of helping young performers. He liked to have many rehearsals—at the rate of one a day—with the soloists present throughout. It was impossible for the stars engaged for the performance to attend such frequent rehearsals so a stand-in system of young talent was used, to such good effect that Klemperer sometimes came to like the stand-in better than the star, and as a result many obtained subsequent engagements and were launched on successful soloist careers.

Although a certain element of luck is involved in getting a break, no one can take advantage of a lucky break and exploit it without being thoroughly prepared. Once again the fundamental advice is 'study the market' and observe yourself constantly in performance—Busoni maintained that no one should live the part completely; five per cent of attention should be detached, observing what is happening. Concentration and attention during practice is vital and will save hours of wasted time and energy. Make the works to be performed your own; know them inside out, backwards, forwards, ill or well, drunk or sober. The audience has paid money to enjoy itself, so manifest your enjoyment in performing; project your performance, unless you intend to be intimate and can compel your audience to come to you, so to speak. There is much to be said for maintaining the atmosphere of magic about music and its performance. Finally, beware of performing without a fee if you wish to be recognised as a professional; give the fee back as a donation in exceptional cases if you wish, but establish your right to a full fee. Never be careless at small or 'unimportant' concerts, there is always someone who knows. Never let someone down because a better date is offered. Many artists do this and managements remember. They also remember, with joy and affection, occasions like that on which Gwyneth Jones, then a young unknown, turned down an offer of a début at Covent Garden to honour a previous engagement to sing in Carol Concerts at the Liverpool Philharmonic, even though the management there offered to release her. It did her career no harm!

Every soloist needs a good agent and manager. This is not just someone who gets you work and looks after your fees, travel, hotels, etc. He should also know your weaknesses and virtues, your level (present and potential), and he should protect you from taking on too many concerts, too many new repertoire works on the one hand, or failure to learn new works on the other, too exhausting a travel schedule and so on.

Many soloists find it very useful, too, to belong to the Incorporated Society of Musicians (not a union) which offers valuable advice on fees, expenses and many other aspects of professional life in an objective manner and enables soloists and private teachers to keep in touch with what is going on in the profession.

When starting out on a soloist's career the main source of engagements will come from the hundreds of music clubs and societies belonging to the National Federation of Music Societies, whose handbook of names and addresses is compulsory reading.

Otto Klemperer conducting the Philharmonia Orchestra in 1972, shortly before his death.

In addition to the BBC and the major orchestras there are hundreds of choral societies, brass bands and other organisations all of whom engage soloists for their concerts; in fact they and the music clubs provide the main source of income for most soloists throughout their careers.

Launching recitals have become very expensive to promote and their chief virtue is that of getting a press notice in one of the national papers, but the number of engagements and the amount of work derived from them is seldom of any real significance. It is far better to seek a début recital under the auspices of the Greater London Arts Association or the Incorporated Society of Musicians, the Kirkman Concerts or one of the many other independent organisations which do such good work in this field.

SECTION III

CHAMBER MUSIC

THE WORLD OF the chamber musician is in many ways very similar to that of the soloist. It is hard to get established and harder still to get to the top. There is a wide gap between the fees that may be earned at one end or the other. It calls for quite exceptional dedication and singleness of purpose and depends almost as much on compatibility of personality as on musical skill. Many young musicians leave college firmly resolved to devote themselves to chamber music; very few do well enough to earn their living at it. But apart from those who get to the very top like the Amadeus Quartet there are many ensembles whose members get enough engagements to give them artistic satisfaction and, by getting in with one of the specialist chamber orchestras also on a regular basis, they make a good living and have an enjoyable life.

One of the most cheering developments of recent years has been the setting up of university quartets and other chamber groups mentioned earlier in the section: Advanced Training—Universities. Many of these ensembles have been established by a combination of the university itself offering free accommodation, concert room and rehearsal rooms; a regional association offering payment for a set number of public concerts in the area; and one of the private trusts (like the Martin Musical Scholarship Fund) making a substantial grant for basic income for the players. In this manner some very fine young quartets have emerged into national recognition—the Fitzwilliam (York and Warwick), the Lindsay (Keele and Sheffield) and the Chilingirian (Liverpool and Sussex) spring immediately to mind.

There is one problem common to both soloists and ensemble musicians: whether to specialise or not. Some have made a career by taking on the difficult, the modern or the unusual repertoire. But it is as easy to become type-cast as it is in the acting profession. At one time Wolfgang Marschner, whose fine violin master classes at Cologne are models for those who seek to develop the classical style of playing, was known in England solely by his ability to play the Schönberg Concerto. Bela Siki, though a beautiful Mozart pianist, was type-cast as a Bartok specialist for years. Offering a speciality is often a way in, so to speak, but, young performers should be aware of its limitations.

COMPOSERS

NEARLY EVERYONE WHO takes up music seriously composes. From the very start many children learning to play an instrument write little pieces for themselves—not perhaps as durable as the works of Mozart, Mendelssohn or Schubert at similar ages, but indicative of as natural an urge to write music as it is for some children to write little stories, once they have learned to read and write.

Composing is a very useful skill to develop, for the purposes of arranging, scoring and many other practical uses, if not for more creative ambitions. A famous soloist once remarked that it was essential to be able to compose in any style in order to keep going during a public performance when he forgot, until he could get in properly again—but he added, 'don't try it with Bach, you'll just get hopelessly lost'.

Apart from following their main study many instrumentalists and singers at music colleges develop their theory lessons into essays in composition. Some, however, take up composition as a main study, developing contacts with established composers and schools of composition within and outside their academic institution. They undertake a long process of learning and individual growth, stretching far beyond student days and they need to take full advantage of all the scholarships, bursaries, travel grants and other facilities offered by the Arts council, the private trusts and by the British Council on behalf of some foreign governments for study abroad (see 'Bridges into the Profession' page 24).

As is the case with conducting, to be considered in the next section, a limited range of skills, of the nuts and bolts variety, can be taught and general influences of style are absorbed from a teacher. But taking up composing as a career makes additional extraordinary demands on a musician in terms of skill, imagination and determination. It is necessary to know the range, sound qualities, technical possibilities and limitations of every instrument and voice; nowadays one must add every electronic device as well. This implies a keen ear and facility in committing to paper what has been perceived in the aural imagination. It is hard enough to devise a good theme, harder still to write a good tune, and yet harder to keep it going and develop it. What is sometimes called musical carpentry in any style still has a place, but that is only the start.

Holst once wrote to his daughter Imogen in a letter: 'You really must waste more paper; to be a composer you must write lots and lots, lots of waste paper before anything can be achieved.'

There is, of course, still a constant demand for all sorts of practical, utility music—for beginners, for schools, for amateur orchestras and choirs, for incidental and background purposes in films, television and radio to mention some obvious outlets.

In more serious areas the world of really modern music has a small but devoted, even passionate, following among the young as is proper in a society that rejects formal patterns and traditions of all kinds, being at once anarchistic and innocent. It would be inappropriate and intrinsically futile to attempt an analysis in this book of anything so fluid and rapidly outdated as contemporary music. The general public may not like or understand it but the would-be-composer must be familiar with the trends whether he uses them in his own composition or not.

In general a career as a composer is for the few. Nothing will stop a musician from persisting with the attempt if the urge is deep enough. Not many will ever reach the position of a Walton, Tippett or Malcolm Arnold, able to devote all their time and energies to composing. It can be argued that composers of all kinds of music, traditional and modern, should continue to be involved in other forms of musical activity—performing or teaching. The development of music departments in universities and polytechnics has helped greatly in this way, the dons having a basic living, opportunities of hearing their works played by the students, vacations long enough for concentrated work, and good contacts with broadcasting and local musical organisations and, even better, with leading musicians from other universities and from abroad. Alexander Goehr at Cambridge, Peter Aston at East Anglia, Alun Hoddinott at Cardiff and David Blake at York are composers who successfully combine university posts with their creative work.

Many more composers teach in schools part-time; some are lucky enough to be offered a post as resident composer like Roger Steptoe at Charterhouse, where he writes his own music and undertakes commissions for groups of boys. On the staff of the BBC there are several established composers who combine their work as producers of programmes with writing music.

In the busy orchestral world such famous conductors as Previn and Bernstein miraculously find time for writing music. So do a number of instrumentalists—Johnny Mayer (violinist), Ray Premru (trombone) and many others combine playing in top orchestras with composing.

Composers can expect to earn something from their compositions, once they become recognised. This will come from commission fees (which may be related to the duration and instrumentation of the work), bursaries from the Arts Council of Great Britain or one of the trusts—the Ralph Vaughan Williams Trust, for instance, favours composers and performances of new music—and from royalties. Music publishers have long acted as agents for the composers whose music they publish, publicising their works in professional circles, but the daunting costs of printing, and the difficulty of getting enough performances to warrant the initial capital outlay, inhibit the production of new music. First performances can be obtained because they do have certain glamorous aspects—'World Premier' for instance always sounds attractive. Second and subsequent performances are more difficult to achieve. Sir Thomas Beecham remarked that the only chance a British composer had of hearing his work twice was in the Albert Hall!

Without a publisher a composer also has the formidable chore of copying score and parts. There are quite a few copyists, but it is boring and taxing work and therefore expensive. One of the objects of the new Hinrichsen Foundation will be to help with copying costs.[1]

---

[1]The Hinrichsen Foundation, 10/12 Baches Street, London N1 6DN or c/o Royal Philharmonic Society, 124 Wigmore Street, London W1.

Composers should belong to the Performing Right Society and the Composers Guild of Great Britain in addition to any other organisation appropriate to their other professional musical life.

Professors Peacock and Weir in their book *The Composer in the Market Place* (Faber Music, 1975) showed that in *median* figures a serious composer earns about ten per cent of his income from composition; sixty-one per cent earned less than twenty per cent, and fourteen per cent earned over eighty per cent from serious composition. Including composers of light and popular music in the calculation the median was thirty-five per cent, but that figure is artificially high on account of the exceptionally high earnings of a very small number of really successful composers.

Experience and statistics seem to reinforce the idea that would-be composers should keep up another money-earning skill, compatible with their creative work, if they are to be financially self-sufficient.

CONDUCTORS

IN MANY WAYS conductors are in a worse position than composers as far as training is concerned. There are certain technical skills which can be taught—score reading, development of a good ear, beating time, instrumentation and transposing instruments, keyboard facility and by no means least—elementary group psychology. But the art of conducting involves a functioning far beyond teachable techniques; it is in a way a mediumistic activity in which the conductor's personal vision of interpretation of a familiar symphony or his aural perception of a new work has to be conveyed so as to ensure unanimity of response by a group of up to a hundred players. He must be aware that these professional players are all, as it were, surrendering their artistic individualities *pro tem*; he must therefore earn their respect by his command of the score musically and technically, and by the overall integrity of the interpretation he is aiming at.

It is sometimes said that conductors fall into two principal categories: first, those who with varying degrees of success impose their will on the orchestra by sheer force of command and technical expertise. Fritz Reiner and George Szell in the past and von Karajan and Maazel in our time rehearse and perform even the most complex works without score, conducting every beat, every demi-semi-quaver with unerring accuracy. Some orchestral players may not like this approach but they respect the masters of it. Farther down the scale there are would-be martinets without the flair or technique who just irritate players.

In the second category are those conductors who (again with more or less success) invite orchestras to make music with them, taking it for granted that the players will look after all the technical bits themselves—Sir Thomas Beecham once described it as 'like riding in the Grand National. You have to assume that you are riding a horse that can jump all the fences'. Cantelli used to look sad if something didn't come off at rehearsal and murmur 'you not suffer enough'; and Klemperer would look surprisedly at the principal of the section concerned in any difficulty and say 'anything wrong Mr X?'

At the lower end of this type of conducting are the sheer incompetents, and in between a large number of conductors whose interesting musical intentions find only occasional expression susceptible of realisation by the players. Toscanini once remarked, 'orchestral players are like peasants who have something hidden in their pockets; you must learn how to make them want to give it to you.'

In the same way that it may be said that there are two types of conductors, it may also be said that they emerge from three main streams of musical activity—orchestral musicians (Giulini, violin; Barbirolli, cello; Colin Davis, clarinet; and Maazel, violin), pianists and opera house repetiteurs (Barenboim, John Pritchard, Bernstein and Previn), and choral scholars and organists (Sir Malcolm Sargent, Sir Charles Groves and Andrew Davis).

There is also the revival of the eighteenth century virtuoso soloist, directing from the solo instrument (Pinchas Zuckerman, Ashkenazy, Menuhin, Tortelier and many others). Many of these superb soloists having reached the pinnacle of success in their own specialisation move over to conducting, spending more and more of their time in this field, thus adding a new dimension to their professional lives.

But whatever his stable or pedigree the life of a professional conductor is hard to establish, though rewarding artistically and financially to the successful ones. It also seems to be a passport to longevity judging by the wonderful span of working life achieved by dozens of the greatest practitioners, from Monteux, Ansermet and Klemperer to Sir Adrian Boult and Karl Böhm. Perhaps this is due to the sheer physical exercise involved in conducting. Sir Geraint Evans, powerfully built though he is, was astounded by the muscular stiffness he suffered during a week of performances of the opera *Il Maestro di Capella* by Cimarosa, in which he had to pretend to conduct as well as to sing. This physical involvement is a marvellous balancing factor for the high degree of cerebral concentration in preparing, memorising and interpreting large-scale works. Perhaps also the variety and volume of work repels the worst ager of all—boredom. Sir Charles Groves, a thoroughly professional musician if ever there was one, has been Principal Conductor and Music Director of the Royal Liverpool Philharmonic Orchestra, and before that of the BBC Northern, the Bournemouth Symphony, the Welsh National Opera and guest conductor regular with the BBC Symphony Orchestra and the Royal Philharmonic Orchestra, and now Music Director of the English National Opera. In all these posts he has planned programmes, auditioned hundreds of soloists, been available for advice to members of his orchestras, advised committees, written articles, broadcast talks, coached young artists at the piano, played chamber music and somehow or other has found time to be a sociable human being, well read, as well informed about politics and sport as about music, and a most excellent companion. No time for boredom for him!

Aspirant conductors will learn quickly for themselves about orchestral attitudes, but they will save themselves much trouble if they always know their work thoroughly before starting rehearsal, avoid sarcasm or picking on individuals in front of the others, honour the proper times for breaks and ending rehearsals, manifest their own integrity *vis à vis* the music, admit their own mistakes without rancour and above all, don't talk too much. Willi Boskowski describes his first rehearsal as leader under Furtwängler: 'He played through the first movement of a Brahms Symphony without stopping; then through the second and then Furtwängler said quite simply *'Bitteschön meine Herren, etwas schöner'* (Please gentlemen, a little more beautifully)'.

The real problem for conductors, as it is for composers, is that they need others for the realisation of their intentions. An orchestra is a very expensive commodity and it is extremely difficult to practise one's art as a conductor without a group of professionals—amateurs need a different approach and technique altogether. There is a limited number of apprenticeship opportunities in England compared say with Germany and its opera houses in every town or with America where many of the great orchestras have one or more young conductors as assistants to their principals. Better schemes of this latter sort are needed in Britain. But meanwhile it is worth noting that there are quite a number of most promising and talented young conductors emerging into the limelight by way of international seminars and competitions, BBC orchestra jobs, private backers and the efforts of individual orchestral managements.

The establishment of more opera companies in Britain provides a new career outlet where conductors can learn their trade thoroughly by working as repetiteurs, chorus trainers and understudies taking over occasional performances. They have to guard against becoming type-cast if they want to develop their main career on the concert platform; the undoubted skills required for holding a complicated work together in the opera house or theatre are not of themselves enough to evoke attention and admiration on the concert platform.

Those who are successful and get an appointment as principal conductor of one of the main regional or BBC orchestras can expect to play an important part in the planning of the overall musical policy and in the development of the orchestra itself, as well as conducting some twenty-five to thirty different programmes (with repeats—fifty to sixty concerts) a year. The door is open for them to receive guest invitations with other orchestras at home and abroad. A good, satisfactory, creative and remunerative life, and the rest is up to them.

One final word of general advice to young conductors. Remember that even your most personal friends assume a different mentality and attitude within the corporate entity of an orchestra at work. And above all make sure everyone knows your detailed rehearsal schedule, when the brass, the harp, the percussion are wanted; exactly what will be rehearsed at a certain time; when the tea break will be (and stick to it); and do invite the principals to advise you on technicalities like bowing, fingering and so on.

SERVICE BANDMASTERS

THE MINISTRY OF Defence Bandmasters Certificate obtained on successful completion of the course at the Royal Military School of Music, Kneller Hall, opens up possibilities of an interesting career first as a warrant officer and later, if the Advanced Certificate is successfully taken, as a candidate for a commission as a director of music.

Even after retirement from the army the training qualifications and experience obtained during service life frequently leads to all manner of interesting jobs in the music profession. Very many valuable recruits to the ranks of professional orchestras and the teaching profession have been obtained from the bandsmen and women who have completed the splendid training available in staff and regimental bands.

A list of Staff and Regimental Bands of the British Army is given in Appendix 11.

ORGANISTS AND CHOIRMASTERS

IT SHOULD BE remembered that the rebirth of professional music-making in Britain was due in large part to the splendid traditions maintained since Tudor times in the cathedrals and churches of the Established Church. They were invigorated late in the eighteenth century by the release of devotional energy in non-conformist churches and chapels following religious emancipation. They flourished particularly in the growing urban industrial areas where in addition to singing in their own services, thousands and thousands of people joined enthusiastically in the performances of quasi-religious oratorios at the flourishing festivals of York, Norwich, Leeds, Birmingham, Manchester, Three Choirs and others too numerous to list.

Organists and choirmasters of every denomination played an inspirational role in this phenomenon. Their professional role as music directors in cathedrals, churches and chapels, great and small, provided them with a relatively modest annual salary, but such appointments carried with them a status with which the holders became local celebrities and musical arbiters as well as securing for them essential extra income from teaching and from professional engagements with choral societies and festivals.

The situation is much the same today. Despite a decline in church- and chapel-going affecting all denominations, our choral traditions still exercise an important part in our local and national musical life. Composers obtain a sizeable proportion of their commissions for church services and choral works, ranging from simple settings of the new vernacular Catholic Mass to massive choral and orchestral works like Tippett's *Vision of St Augustine*. Organists and choirmasters continue to exercise considerable influence with composers and enjoy local standing, a pleasant and musically satisfying life with a decent if not spectacular income.

Those who go into this side of the music profession, learning and nurturing the special skills it calls for, might give particular attention to the technique of conducting a chorus with orchestral accompaniment. After weeks of chorus practices there is normally only one rehearsal with a scratch orchestra with 'professional stiffening' by freelance players, and some choirmasters never succeed in mastering the knack of giving clear indications to the orchestra as well as to the chorus. They often make their task more difficult by choosing programmes which are too long or by putting too many difficult or unfamiliar works in one programme. *These things shall be* (John Ireland), *Five Tudor Portraits* (Vaughan Williams) and *Belshazzar's Feast* (Walton) may seem to be an enterprising programme, but the orchestral problems which will have to be resolved in one rehearsal must also be taken into account. The conductor of a full-time professional orchestra would have at least one, perhaps two, rehearsals with the orchestra alone and at least two with chorus and orchestra.

Young organists and choirmasters should be encouraged to be ambitious but to ensure that they can really handle all the forces of soloists, choir and orchestra at the one joint rehearsal, three hours that often seem like the mad dash of the Grand National field up to the first fences—no fallers please. If continuo parts are to be played on the organ or harpsichord with a professional orchestra it really is wise to be a member of the Musicians Union.

The role of the organist/choirmaster calls for a combination of talents as solo musician, disciplinarian, teacher, arranger, philosopher, and social celebrity. The direct rewards may not match the talents required; but in diffuse and indirect ways, at many different levels, it is a career of great value to the individual and to the community with a host of distinguished names on its Roll of Honour.

ACCOMPANISTS AND REPETITEURS

THIS IS INDEED a wide-ranging branch of the music profession and the skills required of its practitioners are no less wide-ranging. At one extreme there is the rum-ti-tum, 'till ready' type of thing needed for sing-songs and popular ballads for which the pianist should be able to improvise something to go with any simple tune, in any key, and be able also to decorate it with novel touches of his own. At the other artistic pole there are the *Lieder* of Schumann whose accompaniments are virtually piano solos with the singer 'at the voice' quite often. One may be required to play for choral society rehearsals, bringing out one or other of the vocal parts as required; or perhaps to play at concerts for singers who provide tattered copies of the music with the covers missing, and murmur just before you start 'Oh, by the way, put this up (or down) to B flat' or whatever key they reckon will suit their voice. Mind-reading as well as sight-reading, transposition and improvisation are all part of an accompanist's equipment. Keyboard facility is the first essential.

In developing their art accompanists must also learn about many facets of the voices and instruments they are working with at any time. interpretation comes with understanding a singer's approach, knowing the words as well as he does and breathing with him; or knowing the way in which, say, a clarinet speaks with a fractional delay in sound; or how a violinist or cellist must sometimes lift his bow to do two down bows in succession. It is the art of following and, when necessary, leading.

Most accompanists hope to strike up a partnership with a kindred spirit, singer or instrumentalist, and to make such an ensemble the spine of their work. Some develop several such partnerships, but they too are in demand for accompanying auditions, for appearing with young or visiting artists at début recitals and for helping to prepare candidates for major competitions.

In the opera houses the repetiteurs have a wide range of duties, and are much occupied with helping soloists to learn their parts, playing for chorus rehearsals and coaching. Their skills should include playing from a full score, which means playing the relevant bits and missing out many of the lines of the stave.

Although the earnings in this field may never reach the dizzy heights of the international solo pianist there are very good prospects for good musician/pianists and there is always some way of earning one's keep once good connections have been established.

PROFESSIONAL CHORUS SINGERS

THERE IS GOOD demand for singers, especially for tenors, in various types of chorus work. The growth of the professional opera companies has helped very much in this area, and, with the prospects of the English National Opera having a second home in Leeds, and the Welsh National Opera linking with Birmingham, the outlook is even more promising.

For opera chorus work a singer needs a good quality, strong voice, a good physique and appearance and some natural stage instinct. Training in the actual music, make-up, acting and other theatre techniques is provided by production staff within the companies, but it is valuable to get some experience before attempting to join a company. Royal Opera and English National Opera offer full-time salaried contracts; Glyndebourne offers seasonal engagements and the possibility of further engagements with Glyndebourne Touring Opera; the Welsh National Opera and Scottish Opera Companies now also have full-time salaried choruses.

Some opportunities occur for understudying principal roles, but, in general, it is difficult to move across from chorus work into solo parts, and the demands on the voice are not conducive to more refined development. It is a hard life and the remuneration is relatively poor, even on the rates laid down by Equity, to which union all professional chorus singers should belong.

Specialist groups like the BBC Singers, the John Alldis Singers and many other groups need rather different attributes. Certainly they must start with good voices, but physique and appearance are less important than a high musical sense, good ear and excellent sight-reading ability. The BBC Singers are fully employed on salaries. Other groups, including the excellent BBC Northern Singers, are paid fees by the engagement at Equity rates, and many have other occupations, such as teaching, or are embarking on careers as soloists.

Cathedral and church choirs are mostly male singers, lay-clerks, and their stipends are related to a certain number of services each week or month. There is no thought of this representing a living wage, but it is rather an adjunct to whatever they undertake in the realm of music or any other calling as a main means of livelihood. Most such choirs are directly concerned with the Church of England, and although the musical literature is rich, the manner of singing in England tends to be 'churchy' and to militate against the more robust forms of production needed for success as a soloist, although many do get engagements with the choral societies.

It will be appreciated that the vast majority of choral concerts presented in Britain are sung by amateur choral societies, although it is not unknown for them to have a proportion of discreet professional stiffening, among the tenors for instance, for their public performances.

MUSIC PUBLISHING

THERE ARE NOT many openings in the field of music publishing, which requires very astute, highly personal judgement and draws a small number of keen musical brains to exercise their flair—a mixture of business acumen and musical vision. The main music publishers in Britain are listed in Appendix 10.

LIBRARIANSHIP

THIS CAN BE divided into three categories.

1. Unskilled work as library clerks, with a love of and interest in music, is possible to obtain in many local libraries with music sections. Progress depends on the individual's own willingness to study and take librarianship examinations.

2. For the relatively few but excellent music libraries such as the Henry Watson in Manchester, the Picton in Liverpool and the Central Music Library, Westminster, qualified librarians are required who also have specialised musical knowledge.

3. The BBC maintain comprehensive music libraries in London and in the regions, for which the staff need to have more musical knowledge than librarian's qualifications. The same may be said for the major orchestras, all of which maintain a full-time (in the fullest sense of the word!) music librarian responsible for maintaining the orchestra's own library and for obtaining the widest range of music from many different publishers and other sources to meet the requirements and idiosyncracies of their many guest conductors. An orchestral librarian spends much time in marking parts, bowing and so on, and erasing them before returning them to source after use!

RETAIL TRADE

THE DECLINE IN retail music trade is a source of sorrow and discontent among musicians. The inexorable rise in rates, rents and salaries and all overheads, and the logic of the cost accountants have led to the decline of this once flourishing business and useful service. Most of the major music publishers who maintained their own shops in London as an outlet for their wares have closed them. Firms as world famous as W.E. Hill, the luthiers of Bond Street, have moved out of London. In the regions, once great enterprises like Rushworth and Dreaper in Liverpool—organ builders and sellers of music and instruments, who had two recital rooms and studios for practice and teaching—have had to reduce the scale of their musical operations to make room for televisions, radios, music centres,washing machines and other products of the electronics industry. It has become very difficult actually to buy music off the shelf anywhere, with a few honourable exceptions such as the London Music Shop, Blackwells (Oxford) and Banks (York)—one orders it without being able to look at it and then one waits and waits and waits.

Employment in the retail trade is not, alas, to be recommended as a career in Britain any more. We all pray for a revival; but it is difficult to forecast one in a business world dominated by the unwillingness of accountants to accept the old-fashioned principle of overall, rather than itemised profitability.

ADMINISTRATION

THE RANGE OF jobs in musical administration is very wide indeed with a similarly wide variation in the proportions of musical and business management skills and experience needed for their successful accomplishment. It must be said at the outset that there are relatively few jobs at the top, at what might be called general management level and that, although well-paid and absorbingly interesting, they require a dedication as exacting and a flair as great as that exercised by top performers. To run a major opera house or orchestra one must be available day and night, seven days a week. Plans are made and commitments entered into, artistically and financially for three or four years ahead. At the same time an eye has to be kept on day-to-day affairs, on current productions, promotions, hired engagements, foreign tours and recordings, assessing the effects of current experience upon future planning. With this goes the need for sharing the artistic vision of a principal conductor, communicating it a. it were like Aaron to committee members, singers and players and staff, who, one must remember may find it difficult to see beyond the horizons of their own sectional interests. All this is easier said than done when the maintenance of confidentiality in respect of delicate negotiations prevents total openness. One must also deal with the inevitable crises of conductors and soloists being ill, financial anxieties, committee problems and contractual interpretations. One has to be like Father O'Flynn 'checking the crazy ones, coaxing onaisy ones, lifting the lazy ones on with your stick'. As one wife remarked about her husband, manager of a famous orchestra 'You don't manage an orchestra, you marry the blasted thing.'

At different levels administrators need to have some knowledge of and aptitude for three main areas:

1. Business skills—book-keeping and accountancy; statistics and interpretation of trends and tendencies of expenditure and income; company and industrial law; advertising and public relations; printing; insurance; basic sociology and psychology.

2. It is vital to keep observing 'how the machine works'—the structure and mechanics of the unions and the employers' associations; official organisations such as the Arts Council of Great Britain, the British Council, the press, the BBC, local authorities, the recording companies, the colleges of music which are the recruiting grounds for new players—and constantly to watch the

machinery of one's own organisation, to ensure that it is adapted to meet changing circumstances, internal and external, and the needs and well-being of its own playing members and staff.

3. In the directly musical sense, the more one knows about every aspect of music and the profession the better. Certainly one must know where to find the information, either from reference books, catalogues and circulars, or to which of one's colleagues one can turn for reliable advice. The capabilities and fees of hundreds of artists; the current union rates for every type of engagement; instrumentations and timings of works; range of voices; limitations of certain instruments; stage and platform dimensions; transportation of personnel and instruments by road, air, sea or rail; commissioning of music from composers, and of programme notes from musicologists—these are the more obvious matters on which the more knowledge and experience that can be accumulated the better for the manager.

Incidentally although 'quicker reading' methods have their dangers and limitations, they do enable administrators to scan through the vast amount of circulars and leaflets they receive, addressed to them, not for direct action on their part but for information in the broadest sense. It's amazing how a bit of information one has gleaned unconsciously from a quick reading of some such document, floats back usefully to the surface in some quite different context. This knack applies particularly to employment in large organisations, the BBC for instance, when the system depends on vast circulation of copies.

It would be misleading to attempt to give any indication of potential earnings in the administrative areas of music in any detail. Suffice it to say that as things are, and as they are likely to remain in the foreseeable future, incomes at general management levels are very much higher than those only a little further down the scale in the orchestral and recording worlds, which nevertheless still seem to exercise a Lorelei spell to lure young men and women from more lucrative commercial employment onto the rocks of a career still enveloped in mist.

In opera houses and all the official organisations a much better grading has been achieved; those in the middle echelons of management are able to earn a relatively good living.

The following is a guide to the main areas and categories of employment in the administration of music.

THE ARTS COUNCIL OF GREAT BRITAIN is the official organisation set up by the government for the administration of central public funds for the arts. The major administrative positions within this organisation are:

Music Director; Deputy Music Director; and several specialist assistants.

There is also a director responsible for all touring companies, theatrical, operatic and musical.

In the main the Arts Council does not initiate musical activity or promote concerts. It works in response to the policies and initiations of the organisations it helps in an advisory, consultative and supervisory role. The Council does play a more direct part in the field of new music; commissions and bursaries to composers have become an increasingly important part of its work, although the proportion of money spent in this area still appears tiny compared with the vast sums allocated to performing organisations such as opera companies and orchestras.

THE BRITISH COUNCIL'S officers overseas are mainly concerned with educational aspects of the arts, but many have some training in music and they play a large part in co-ordinating the tours of British soloists, ensembles, orchestras and opera companies in the countries in which they are serving.

The Head of Music of the British Council in London and his small staff play a very important and interesting part in helping individuals, groups and companies to tour overseas, either financially or with advice and practical help such as introductions.

THE MUSICIANS UNION officials are mostly drawn from the ranks of its own members.

All the other organisations listed in Appendix 13 are administered by relatively small expert staffs.

CONCERT HALL MANAGEMENT. The South Bank Concert Hall complex, Royal Festival Hall, Queen Elizabeth Hall and Purcell Room, is managed by a large staff, all GLC employees but recruited from a big range of musical backgrounds. Fairfield Hall at Croydon, the Barbican Arts Centre of the Future, Royal Albert Hall, Wigmore Hall and many concert halls all over the country offer a considerable number of jobs in which men and women of a practical turn of mind may put their musical education to good use.

THE BBC has its major radio music division in London with a large department in Manchester and sizeable staffs also in Birmingham, Cardiff, Glasgow and Belfast. Employment in music with the BBC falls into five main categories:

1. *Programme producers*—responsible for devising and producing broadcast programmes within set artistic and budget policies.
2. *Studio managers and engineers*—vital and interesting roles including balancing sound, score reading and many technical skills.
3. *Orchestral management*—as well as the BBC Symphony Orchestra there are the Concert Orchestra in London, the BBC NSO, BBC SSO and the BBC Welsh and Northern Ireland orchestras.

The South Bank Concert Halls—Royal Festival Hall, Queen Elizabeth Hall and Purcell Room.

4. *Librarians*—in addition to the chief music librarian and his staff in London each of the other main centres has its own music librarian.

5. *Senior management*—responsible for a wide range of planning and organisation. The Controller of Music and his main planning assistants in London, helped by the Heads of Music in the Regions, control the output of programmes in close contact with the Controller of each of the services and their staffs.

Music for BBC television is organised separately with a Head of Arts and Music Programmes with planning assistants and several programme producers. By their nature TV programmes are more complex than those for radio and take much longer to plan and to produce! A radio producer may be responsible for up to a hundred programmes a year; a TV producer for a quarter of that number.

All posts in the BBC are on the official scales and conditions of service laid down in a comprehensive system of grading.

RECORD COMPANIES. Apart from top management and marketing most jobs are as producers and engineers, all of whom have to have a keen ear, good judgement and an ability to read scores. (See Appendix II.)

ORCHESTRAS. Most orchestras operate with very small staffs indeed compared with their continental counterparts in say, Germany, where there are research assistants, archivists and other experts; or in the USA, where essential public relations and fund-raising operations result in total staffs of between fifty and sixty in Chicago, Boston and similar orchestras. The usual in Britain is about eight to ten, i.e. general manager, deputy, concerts manager, publicity and printing officer, finance officer, with up to five secretaries and junior assistants. The orchestra manager, librarian and transport officer are usually reckoned as technical ancillaries of the orchestra itself rather than as administrative staff.

Some of the smaller irregular orchestras may operate with only two or three staff doing everything themselves.

REGIONAL ARTS ASSOCIATIONS. The Regional Arts Associations listed in Appendix 6 derive their income in part from the Arts Council of Great Britain and in part from the local authorities in the area of their operations. They may also seek sponsorship from industry and commerce, usually for specific activities. In general they do not promote musical events directly, but they operate through existing concert societies and music clubs (or persuade independent groups of people to set them up), responding to and stimulating local demand. Although they are the channel through which Arts Council subventions reach many of the smaller organisations in the regions, the major orchestras, theatres and festivals still deal direct with the Arts Council—a weakness in that it diminishes the Arts

Associations' local importance; an advantage in that they avoid the criticism that would ensue if a major proportion of their grants went to one or two large companies.

Each of the Regional Arts Associations has a director and several specialist assistants, including one for music. These posts are paid on grades and scales related to local authority grades in the area. See Appendix 6 for names and addresses of Regional Arts Associations.

LOCAL AUTHORITIES in many parts of Britain have developed their own direct provision of entertainment. The range of these activities varies greatly, but quite a number of posts have been set up as music assistants to entertainment or amenity officers. They are well paid by standards in other types of arts administration and appointments are made on local authority grades and rates of pay.

FESTIVALS such as the Edinburgh Festival or the Aldeburgh Festival engage staff on a full-time basis all the year round. The smaller festivals may have a part-time director or secretary all the year round. Both types rely heavily on students and enthusiasts for the few weeks prior to the festival and for the period of the festival itself. Each festival is so individual that it is impossible to generalise about pay and conditions of work, except to say that for the temporary ancillaries there is more to be gained in the way of the experience, and the contacts with artists at all levels to be enjoyed, than in any real monetary reward.

ARTISTS' AGENTS AND CONCERT MANAGEMENTS. For a comprehensive view of the whole musical performers' profession there are few jobs to compare with that of the artists' agent or manager. He must know the whole musical scene locally, nationally and internationally. He must keep abreast of public taste, and anticipate and influence the directions it might take. He must have close links with hundreds of music clubs and societies and their local officials, as well as commanding the respect of the managers of the major orchestras, operas and choral societies. He must gauge the sort of fees that are obtainable from many different promoters for the artists he is representing. He acts as a travel bureau, hotel guide and general factotum for his artists. He often undertakes promotions of concerts himself at his own risk, sometimes recitals, sometimes concertos with orchestra. He deals and makes contracts with recording companies, the BBC and ITV. In short he has to command a wide range of detailed knowledge, keep good relations with a vast number of influential officials in many different fields, be able to assess the real quality and potential of the artists he represents and have a keen nose for new ideas and developments.

Nowadays some agents work on a fixed management fee, determined annually, for each of their artists; most charge a percentage of every fee earned (usually 15 per cent) with adjustments for, say, conductors or opera singers on continuing contracts. An agent, therefore, needs a nucleus of strong, high-fee-earning artists to be able to meet the high costs of office accommodation in London, of postage, of telephone services (many intercontinental calls), of expert advice on tax matters and similar problems, as well as of entertaining. As in any other business the knack is knowing how many artists one can cope with on a certain level of staffing, and, of these, how many young unknowns one can afford to nurture, since the expenses involved in every sale, so to speak, are disproportionately high and the fees earned inversely low for the unknown.

However, agents offices, low paying though they may be, provide a wonderful training ground for young administrators, giving them a detailed insight into the whole business. To set up as an independent agent or to go into partnership with an established one requires a substantial outlay of capital. (See List of Agents in Appendix 13.)

In any branch of administration and at every level several important faculties should be nurtured and cultivated. First the quality of leadership, with a range of background knowledge born of personal experience, and keen intuition about the future, and the instinct by which new talent is spotted—anyone can say that Rubinstein or Menuhin are great artists; the one who spots their successors is the genius.

You must get to know how the machine works, every part of it. Don't let it eat you up; but don't break parts of it in getting your own way—once damaged the machine won't work for you again.

Admit your own mistakes—to yourself, to others, senior, equal or junior—admit them; others will respect you for it and will help you. One or two may try to trip you up, but if you admit your own errors quickly and ungrudgingly you are on firm ground. The difference between the general manager of an orchestra and, say, its principal horn, is that a couple of bubbles or breaks will earn a bad notice in the press for all to read, even damning the whole orchestra such as 'Whatever has happened to the standard of the Philharmonia?' (an actual headline some years ago). The general manager, on the other hand, even on a good day may find that five per cent of his decisions are based on errors of judgement. The following day, however, he can put most of those errors right by admitting them.

Above all, play fair. Even a hard disciplinarian will be respected if he is manifestly fair in all his dealings with everyone.

EXAMINERS AND ADJUDICATORS

THE VALUE FOR pupil and teacher alike of preparing for and taking the graded examinations of the Associated Board, or one of the other official bodies, was stressed earlier. To justify the confidence placed in these examinations, large numbers of experienced musicians willing to devote a part of their normal busy lives as teachers or performers are needed and the demand for them gets bigger and bigger as the world-wide number of candidates grows. Examiners have to combine an intimate knowledge of the academic requirements of each grade with some understanding of the technical particularities of the instruments (or voices) they are listening to, be accurate in marking and above all have an instinct for making the sort of general comments in their reports which will encourage both teacher and pupils by making points of a positive character. Quite often such points are the very ones the teacher has been trying to get across to the pupil and reinforced in this way they may be taken to heart.

It is an exacting task, with long hours, not always the most pleasant rooms for the auditions, and occasional dry spells as far as talent is concerned. Tours of the major centres abroad, in Australia, Hong Kong, Canada and other overseas centres are a wonderful experience but they last for several weeks, even months and the schedule is a hard one with long distances to travel, arduous days and nights of generous but often exhausting hospitality in areas in which the visitor is a celebrity from the wider world, whose visit is the musical event of the year and whose presence is, therefore, to be made the most of socially.

The fees to be earned are not high but, of course, all expenses are met. The contact with young musicians of the future and their teachers is stimulating and the thrill of the occasional revelation of real musical gifts is only matched by the satisfaction of witnessing later its full flowering in maturity.

Similar patterns of work can be expected by adjudicators, again not a full-time occupation, but one which is a useful adjunct to the normal teaching or performing life of its practitioners. The festivals at which they operate are organised by local committees of amateur enthusiasts, often the parents of musical children and one or more local teachers, and always with the inevitable enthusiastic secretary and chairman. They spend most of their free time organising the events, booking halls, arranging publicity, pianos and adjudicators, raising money and dealing with applications from competitors.

This too is an exacting and exhausting task for the visiting musicians. Three sessions a day of three hours each, hearing perhaps up to forty performances of the same piece, making a public adjudication, announcing the winners and giving constructive assessments at the end of every class (and sometimes getting a hostile reception from the audience, which at least demonstrates their active interest)—in two or three days at a festival an adjudicator certainly earns the quite modest fees that are paid. However, like examining, the delight of hearing, say, a class of young violinists all manifesting the work of an outstanding teacher in the district by their stance, or bowing, or clean intonation, is immeasurable, as is the joy of spotting someone who is really going to 'make it'.

Although concerned with accuracy in performance, adjudicators are less tied to academic aspects of appraisal than examiners: in the final analysis it is performing potential that really counts in this area.

TEACHING MUSIC

TEACHING AT ALL levels represents the seed bed which will determine the strength, variety and quality of the future plants. By means of the most elementary lessons at school interest in music can be awakened in the very young by teachers with affection and enthusiasm for the subject; potential talent can be spotted and encouraged by teachers of discernment; indeed at every stage and level of development of student life the teacher plays a vital role.

Doubts are sometimes expressed as to whether teachers are properly prepared for their special roles in every area of their occupation. It used to be asserted by cynics that the teaching profession was the last resort of failed performers. Thanks to the post-war growth of provision for instrumental lessons in schools such a charge would have minimal application nowadays, as many instrumental teachers have experience as professional orchestral players, either on a freelance basis or as former members of full-time orchestras with plenty of experience in, and continuing contacts with, the performing profession. In any case it might well be argued that in an ideal situation all teachers should do some professional performing and all performers should do some teaching. The romantic notion of the virtuoso soloist of the nineteenth century was perhaps an unbalanced phenomenon, and a return to the natural versatility of all artists cultivated in earlier times is to be encouraged and desired.

Nevertheless, doubts are voiced, not least by young teachers themselves as to whether more could and should be done at music colleges, universities and colleges of education to prepare students more effectively for the situation in which they will find themselves in any branch of the teaching profession—positive preparation factually and in mental attitude. In respect of the music colleges the Gulbenkian Report includes some definite proposals for having a number of different courses open to students more directly suited to career needs:

(a) the normal performers course should be reduced to two years with the second stage of training in an in-service situation with an orchestra, for instance. Performers wishing to take a degree for teaching purposes should have a four year course;

(b) special provision should be made for those going in for instrumental teaching but wishing to attain higher levels of personal performance;

(c) similar provision should be made for university graduates seeking advanced performance standards;

(d) class teachers wishing to improve their instrumental skills to enable them to teach instruments as well should be catered for.

Whether these and other recommendations are accepted and acted upon or not, there is no doubt that the functions of the various institutions involved in the training of teachers will be under close scrutiny by the government and local authorities concerned and by the students themselves in the light of the major cuts in financial allocations and the severe reduction in the number of places available at colleges of education and polytechnics.

To describe the many branches of the teaching side of music would need a book to itself, a separate book for each branch in fact. All that is attempted here is an identification of the principal areas, with short notes on the qualifications needed, some idea of career prospects, and some general notes on the nature of the work and the conditions, under the main headings of: Music teachers in schools; Private teachers; Music Colleges and Schools of Music; Universities and Polytechnics.

MUSIC TEACHERS IN SCHOOLS

Music in schools falls into three main areas: general class teaching; instrumental teaching; and teaching in music centres.

Teachers for general class teaching, which in larger schools with keen musical interest will probably involve several members with a head of department, are recruited from universities, colleges of education and the music colleges. Some will have had direct training for the school life as their main course; some will have taken a Dip.Ed. to supplement their degree in music or whatever their principal study was, and this is now a requirement for new entrants.

Instrumental teachers will have had more advanced performer's training, many will have done some professional orchestral work, and although all should have some preparation for school work with or without an academic qualification for it, the emphasis for instrumental teachers will be on practical aspects of playing.

Teachers at music centres will be drawn from both the above categories, with the addition of private teachers and other professionals not involved in school teaching normally.

Anyone who has done any class-teaching or demonstrating instruments in schools will know that the first essential is being able to keep order. Teachers may achieve this, rather like the case of conductors described earlier, with greater or lesser degrees of success by two methods (each *con variazioni*). The first is by imposing their will and discipline upon the class from the outside, so to speak; the second by securing the attention of the class through making the subject really interesting and obtaining the involvement and co-operation, at least of the majority. There will nearly always be a few disrupters of either method, but the majority will usually follow the teacher once his or her authority has been established. This can only be achieved by teachers who know their subject thoroughly and know how to make lessons interesting. It is essential to keep one step ahead of the class and that is quite a trick to master with pupils absorbing material and responding at different *tempi*. Once the class as a group has drawn level, the direction of attention changes and not many teachers will be able to catch up again during that lesson, at least not without a disproportionately great effort.

The parallel with the orchestra/conductor relationship is not as far-fetched as it may seem. Despite the orchestra's apparent maturity, difference of purpose, professional pride and need to earn money, orchestral players, too, have familiar group reactions. Many a conductor with good musical ideas has lost control of an orchestra and of a rehearsal by concentrating too often or too long on the problems of the strings, bowing, fingering etc., leaving the woodwind and brass with far too much time to read newspapers, play music-stand chess or to initiate out of boredom one of the many tactics of musical gamesmanship guaranteed to wreck serious rehearsal. Or again, a conductor can lose all by picking on an individual, say a horn or clarinet, at first boring, then irritating, and finally exasperating, the whole group. Similar hazards await the teacher. Even exceptional musical skills will not suffice to hold a class together if a teacher hasn't grasped the extraordinary phenomenon of group mentality and behaviour, which occurs in any organised field, commercial and industrial as well as artistic.

Much depends on the attitude of the head of any school in terms of discipline and the encouragement or otherwise of music, or any other 'fringe' subject. Many a peripatetic teacher has learned to discern the main characteristics of the head of a school before meeting him or her personally, simply from the general attitude of the rest of the staff and of the pupils, and from the prevailing atmosphere. There are schools in which a master or mistress stands at the end of every second or third row 'keeping order' during a concert-cum-demonstration of instruments, effectively obliterating any possibility of a natural response from the children. At the other extreme there are schools where no one seems to be in charge and the visiting teacher wastes most of the period establishing some sort of order in the class.

General class-music teachers should have a reasonable key-board facility and be able to play for school assembly, class singing and pupils' concerts; they should have a sound elementary conducting technique for choir and, in bigger schools, orchestra training. They have to teach theory of music, harmony, melody and form, also history of music. They must take musical appreciation with the aid of records, cassettes and the splendid broadcast programmes devised for schools. With luck they may be called upon to take pupils to public concerts by professional orchestras, which in the regions particularly have a regular place in the schedules of the orchestras concerned in co-operation with the local education authorities and involve preparation by the teachers as part of their class work. Music teachers in this category are paid at Burnham Scale rates appropriate to their qualifications and grades of appointment. There are possibilities of promotion within the school system itself, perhaps to the headship of a music department in a bigger school or with responsibility for 'O' and 'A' level examination preparation, or perhaps to a post as music adviser or organiser to an education authority or to one as an inspector of music for the Department of Education and Science.

Visiting teachers are concerned with instrumental teaching, mainly by group teaching methods—an expertise in itself. They organise orchestral practice, advise on advanced lessons for individual students, help with demonstrations of instruments and with pupils' concerts and should be able to play at a high level themselves as soloists. Peripatetic teachers too are mostly engaged on a salaried basis, or on *ad hoc* fees related to such rates, at Burnham Scales, plus allowances for travelling. They have the advantage in many cases of centrally organised supplies of instruments, music and equipment to draw upon. Relatively few are left on the old basis of the pioneering days of school instrumental teaching in the post-war 1940s when a teacher might get at best five or six periods a week at widely separated schools, searching junk shops in their own time for cheap violins, bows and strings for their classes. It may be timely at this point to urge upon everyone concerned with this work, heads, class teachers and visiting teachers, the need to have proper storage facilities and maintenance routines for instruments; often, alas, the lack of care by those in charge is reflected in the cavalier manner in which such expensive instruments and equipment are treated by students.

The link between the general class music teacher and the visiting peripatetic instrumental specialist plays an important part in the success or otherwise of the system. In some schools, because there is a keen music teacher on the staff and because the head backs the scheme, the visiting teacher finds everything laid on—a room allocated, pupils ready with their instruments, stands amd music, and all the co-operation which ensures that everyone gains the maximum benefit from the visit. Plans for school concerts can be discussed; external exams for individual pupils can be considered; visits to competitive and other festivals, to youth orchestras and advanced classes can be arranged. The occasional lack of such obvious elementary co-operation prompted the Gulbenkian Report Committee to stress the need for establishing the responsibility of the resident general music teacher to afford proper liaison and make all necessary contacts within the school for visiting teachers.

Music centres, upon which so much hope is being pinned for the provision of better facilities for talented children in the future, function mostly at weekends, drawing heavily on the services of the peripatetic instrumental teachers, any private teachers and active orchestral players available, as well as on some of the school music staff. Many private teachers encourage their own pupils to attend the centres to give them a chance of rubbing shoulders with boys and girls from other schools. Apart from the full-time staff on appropriate salary scales, payment of fees to other teachers is made on an *ad hoc* basis linked to local authority rates. One glaring anomaly remains to be resolved in the field of casual teaching under local education authority auspices. As things stand an excellent string player with years of experience in one of the great orchestras, may if 'unqualified' get a lower grade of pay than a teacher who may be inferior in every respect but who happens to have taken an examination at college which gives him a graduate rating. One sees the difficulty of qualitative choice that selection procedures would involve in the absence of paper qualifications. But the shortage of good string teachers is so acute that some system of competence should be worked out without delay to capture for this work the many expert orchestral players, married ladies and retired players and others whose influence could be invaluable, but who are currently handicapped because in their college days, being destined to become performers, they did not take the extra examinations conferring graduate status.

PRIVATE MUSIC TEACHERS

As mentioned earlier, the category of private music teacher embraces everyone from the great international virtuoso, whose part in it in modern times is mostly in the form of master classes (preferably in liaison with the regular teachers of the participants) and top pedagogues like Galamian in New York for violinists, Fanny Waterman in Leeds for pianists, and Nadia Boulanger in Paris for composers and keyboard interpretation, right through the whole scale to Mr X or Miss Y in very modest conditions who advertise 'vacancies for piano pupils' and who sometimes take up to sixty or seventy pupils a week at very cheap rates to make ends meet.

There is little real proof of qualifications or teaching ability at either extreme. The letters after the name of the pianoforte teacher in Laburnum Grove may indicate nothing more than that the holder did have some lessons and took some exams; or they may be evidence of a thorough musical training. Similarly the famous player, the virtuoso, may not have any gift for teaching or may delegate actual tuition to one of his other pupils, to the grave disappointment of advanced students who were expecting more direct contact with the master; or the star may be one of that long and distinguished line of great musicians who find inspiration for themselves as well as providing it by having a group of young players around them. The problems of finding the right teacher at any stage of development was mentioned in Chapter I.

However, there are hundreds and hundreds of fine teachers, including many who, in addition to being on the staffs of the music colleges for a certain number of periods each week, devote the rest of their time to teaching privately. Frequently they will prepare young pupils over several years to the point at which they leave school and continue their studies and this close relationship with the same teacher at one of the colleges.

Private teaching, at whatever level it is undertaken and whatever the fees charged, is a hard life calling for great patience, skill and dedication on the part of its practitioners. Private teachers need to know how to help pupils and their parents to get grants from local education authorities and from trusts and scholarship funds. They must keep their own books straight, not forgetting income tax and in many cases VAT. They have to keep a firm grip on those who fail to turn up for lessons or who cancel without adequate notice; and conversely they have to make up for any lessons lost through their own fault; all sets of lessons should be paid for in advance, hence the mutual obligation. They have to assist with advice on the purchase of instruments and music; secure the parents' co-operation over practice; know all the regulations and requirements of the Associated Board and similar graded exams; spend much time thinking about the personal difficulties and strengths of each pupil and prepare all lessons individually. It is an honourable and indispensable branch of the music profession and many a fine musician can attribute much of his later success to the skill and devotion of his early teacher, one of the many whose names may not be recorded in the annals of fame.

Some private teachers play an important part as visiting instrumental specialists in the school system or at music centres. But working on one's own so much makes it imperative to belong to one or more of the various professional organisations listed in Appendix 13 which provide contact with other teachers and a whole range of valuable advice on musical techniques, repertoire and many business and practical matters.

TEACHERS IN MUSIC COLLEGES AND SCHOOLS OF MUSIC

Traditionally the music colleges and schools of music have drawn their staff mainly from the ranks of private teachers, members of orchestras and opera companies and the world of cathedral and church organists and choirmasters together with their associations with many distinguished composers. Apart from a limited establishment of permanent members of staff—the principal, the director of studies, the bursar and the administrator with their assistant staffs—most of the professors and other teachers are remunerated on a fee per student basis. The fees are low, especially in London, and it is not uncommon for a professor to find one of his recent students earning at a much higher rate per hour in a school teaching post. The Royal Northern College of Music solved this problem at the time of the amalgamation of the former Royal Manchester College of Music with the Northern School of Music. The new foundation was created under the auspices of four major local authorities and, though losing some degree of independence, it gained conditions of work for its staff and a new purpose-built School of Music far beyond anything that can be achieved privately in modern times. The consortium of local authorities did in fact permit the retention of several sources of special funds to use for extra-curriculum purposes. In London the Guildhall school of Music and Drama, with its formal links with the City of London Corporation, also enjoys a more direct form of support than the other colleges, and the Royal Scottish Academy of Music is financed directly by the Scottish Department of Education.

The Gulbenkian Report recommends better conditions for the staffs of London colleges, on the lines of those prevailing in the Royal Northern College where a rate of over twice the London rate is paid, and staff are engaged on a salaried basis *pro rata* for the number of days per week they teach.

The title 'professors' is freely used at music colleges, but it does not have the significance of the same title at universities, where it represents a specific standing and function, e.g. the incumbent of the Chair of Music. Perhaps the use in music colleges has its origin in the Italian *'I Professori'*, meaning literally the professionals (members of the orchestra for instance) who are also teachers. Most of the professors teach only two or three days a week at college; most of their work is done privately. Senior students help with teaching in the colleges' junior schools (Saturdays); some graduate into taking second study students in the college itself; some go on to become members of the staff.

However, as has already been explained, most of the instrumental teaching, other than piano, is done by members of the orchestras, indisputably *I Professori*, and soloists. The demands of their professional work sometimes makes lessons irregular, but by and large the system works well, to the mutual advantage of students and teachers.

It might be fair to say in summary that teaching at a college of music is not so much a career in itself as an adjunct of greater or lesser importance of a career in another field, as a composer, performer or private teacher.

TEACHERS IN UNIVERSITIES AND POLYTECHNICS

To teach at a university as lecturer, senior lecturer, reader or professor one needs high academic qualifications, although occasionally distinguished achievement in the sphere of musical research or letters attracts an invitation to a Chair such as Gerald Abraham graced at Liverpool in the 'fifties. Frequently the pattern is that of an outstanding graduate with a first class honours degree being encouraged and financed to continue with postgraduate research, thus securing a foothold on the academic ladder. It is a valuable situation for composers or for those wishing to pursue musicology or for those undertaking research for the purpose of producing performing editions of lost or neglected music. It gives opportunities for performing, conducting, arranging music and for taking full advantage of the facilities provided by universities and of the skills and versatility of staff and undergraduates there.

The salary scales show big differentials between lecturers at the start of their careers and their senior colleagues who at the top of the scale earn twice as much as those at the bottom, a range of £3,000–£6,000 in 1977. Readers may earn up to thirty per cent more than top lecturers, and professors usually receive twenty-five per cent more than that; but there is considerable variation in the top rates as between universities.

Polytechnics and colleges of education, although having a somewhat different emphasis in their functioning, with a more directly teacher-production bias, may be considered as similar in the context of the academic qualifications required for appointments. There is not such a wide differential in their salary scales, which tend to have a higher starting point for lecturers with a lower ceiling at the top.

It is worth repeating for the benefit of all who make a career of teaching music, whether privately, in schools, colleges of music or universities, that they should keep up their own music-making, combined with the best lessons they can get for themselves, whatever the instrument or voice. This is the best way of keeping fresh and alert for the task of teaching.

MUSICOLOGISTS AND CRITICS

THE BASIC QUALITY for anyone wanting to make a career from writing about music is a flair for writing; not such an obvious statement as it might seem. No matter how original a piece of research, nor how accurate an assessment of a new work or of a performance, the end product depends for its effectiveness upon being readable. This flair for writing must be backed by other qualities. Critics should have a real love of music, strong enough to survive years of performances of familiar works without ever losing the sensation of respect for the music or of the delight of those who are hearing the works for the first time. They should have a sympathetic understanding of performers; a sound grasp of the history of music and the principles of the art form; and how wonderful if, too, they possess that insight and innate generosity of spirit which prompted Schumann (who was also a writer as well as a composer) to write after his first hearing of a work by the then young, unknown Chopin, 'Hats off, gentlemen, a genius'. What a contrast to the predicament of Bruckner who begged the Vienna Philharmonic not to give the first performance of his Seventh Symphony because Hanslick would tear it to pieces; rather let Leipzig have the first hearing, where it would be assessed more objectively.

Newspaper critics write mainly for the sizeable public interested in music, both concert-goers and the even larger body of listeners to broadcast concerts and recordings; at best they also reach the general public to some extent. Neville Cardus wrote of Sam Langford of the (Manchester) *Guardian:* 'Everybody knew him . . . university professors, crossing sweepers, prelates and publicans, cab drivers and carriers in the market called him Sammy. His articles were cut out and pasted into albums in remote fastenesses of the North by that now extinct school of workers and thinkers who tried to build Jerusalem amongst the dark satanic mills . . .'.

Musicologists, however, write mainly for a much smaller circle of those with interest in specialist subjects, research and deeper examination of musical matters. They too need to write well, for it is all too easy to lose interest in a work of profound erudition if it is dully written. It is not suggested that these fields of criticism and musicology are mutually exclusive for their practitioners. Many critics write books on significant musical matters and contribute articles to learned journals; and many musicologists cover concerts and provide record reviews and articles for popular periodicals. The distinction is drawn to illustrate the professional outlook for those who feel drawn to a career in this area. Where, however, is their basic income going to come from?

With few exceptions musicologists will be employed in the academic orbit, in a teaching post at a university, technical college or school. Some may find work corresponding to their expertise in the BBC—one thinks immediately of Hans Keller, Basil Lam, Robert Layton, Stephen Plaistow and Nicholas Kenyon to name a few whose contributions are a regular feature of newspapers, journals and magazines. Whether as lecturers, teachers or radio producers, musicologists get from their main employment their basic income and facilities for study, research and contacts; their writing, though an important part of their whole musical life, is a source of occasional jam rather than bread and butter.

Critics on the other hand are basically journalists and those writing for the major newspapers enjoy all the benefits won for journalists in recent years by their professional organisations. By comparison with many other branches of the musical profession considered in this book they do well in terms of salary, expenses and opportunities for other forms of writing. Fees for casual articles are not so good. Many get interesting assignments abroad to cover festivals, opera and tours of British orchestras. Critics must have a good score-reading ability, some real knowledge and understanding of the particularities and peculiarities of voices and instruments, and a taste for evening work with deadlines for their papers and battles with sub-editors over headlines, which they share with their fellow journalists in news of all kinds.

Perhaps it's not quite so hectic as in former days, described by Neville Cardus in his Autobiography, when all copy was written on the tram going back to the offices after a concert and when a notice of only 600 words would bring a reprimand from the editor. One suspects that much of the meat about the music was written before the concert and the report on the ephemeral performance were the bits filled in on the tram, for the writing in those days was extremely good and still most entertaining to read.

Critics like Ernest Newman in his later years writing for the *Sunday Times* had more time to ponder and refine his articles, most of which dealt with serious and weighty matters, as did his lengthy controversy with Shaw about Wagner.

But about the time that the vogue for aleatoric music began (music in which the performer is left to improvise or fill out parts of a work within the framework of general indications set out by the composer) and the cult of longer and longer silences developed, Newman wrote a long article called the 'Silent Symphony'. In it he recounted the saga of the Arab philosopher whose life was devoted to collecting holes in the desert; he dreamed of the day when he would find a hole so immense that there would be nothing surrounding it. Newman thought the idea should be extended to modern music with a silence so long that there would be no sounds to spoil it.

Music critics today write in very different conditions, not only for themselves as journalists, but also for readers. The different modes of transport to and from work now used by millions—the car instead of the tram, train or bus, the availability of instant news on transistor radio and television, the general atmosphere of rush—all combine against the more expansive forms of journalism, and incidentally have led to the demise of many papers once renowned for their arts notices. Nevertheless, it is an encouraging phenomenon that a taste for the delights of music is spreading to an ever larger and wider public than in earlier times by means of radio, records and cassettes and through the much greater availability of live concerts. There is a corresponding desire to know more about the art, and it is up to writers and broadcasters to convince managers, editors and planners of all the media that the market for information and intelligent communication on all arts matters is much more widely based than they have yet realised.

The last word on the subject must be Shaw's. He wrote for the *Scottish Musical Monthly* in 1894 an article 'How to become a Musical Critic', from which the following is an excerpt:

> My own plan was a simple one. I joined the staff of a new daily paper as a leader writer. My exploits in this department spread such terror and confusion that my proposal to turn my attention to musical criticism was hailed with inexpressible relief, the subject being one in which lunacy is privileged. . . .
> I wrote every week on Music, the first condition of which was that it should be attractive to the general reader, musician or non-musician . . .

CONCLUSION

IT CANNOT BE repeated too often or stressed too much that all musicians in any field of the profession must study the market. Whether as a composer, performer, teacher, or administrator, whatever your branch of the profession you must create a demand for what you have to offer, what is particular to you. Study the market thoroughly and constantly to spot where you might be able to sell your talents and to discover how you might be able to direct your talents to meet some existing need or how you might create a demand.

Art, including the performing, teaching and administrating side, should be creative, a synthesis, a bringing together of sometimes seemingly disparate or unrelated ideas or views. Analysis has its place and function, but a taking to bits should never be attempted without the purpose, time and ability for a reassembling. How many conductors fail at rehearsal through wanting to change too much in a familiar work in order to give it their personal interpretation and end up like Humpty Dumpty.

Never stop learning from great masters and remember you can often learn from an indifferent performance or interpretation. Frank Titterton used to practise mimicking singers with production faults and by this means he could work out what they were doing wrong and thus be able to help them at lessons.

Avoid mannerisms, grimaces, fidgeting, swaying and ballet movements—practice in front of a mirror helps to check incipient bad habits.

Practise performing—to anyone. The sensation and experience of performing is quite different to private practice and is a skill to be worked at.

Build a repertoire carefully; make sure it suits your talents and beware of works that are not within the range of your technique or sympathies. Be very wary about the inclusion of too many new pieces in your programme for the same concert, however well they have gone in private practice; bring them in one or two at a time, well supported by works you have performed often.

Practise walking on and off a platform, stance and posture while performing, and acknowledgement of applause. In *The Art of Singing* Plunkett Greene wrote: 'the manner of your entrance onto the platform determines the first few minutes of your performance; if you muff it or fail to get the attention of your audience you have to spend the first ten minutes in actual performance working extra hard to recapture their interest.'

Make sure you have an up-to-date world-wide insurance policy to cover your instruments in every situation and have them revalued regularly; take out *full* insurance cover against sickness and accident when working abroad.

All the mundane details should be checked; time of rehearsal, the place, music stands, piano tuning, every detail should be checked and not left to your memory. The same applies to administrators going to meetings, lecturers and teachers taking classes—check time, place, documents, books, records tapes, anything you may require.

In one of the essays in *Points of View* T.S. Eliot wrote, 'It is said that the dead writers are so remote from us because we *know* so much more than they did—precisely, and *they* are that which we know. So how much more are we in our turn going to add to that succession of increased knowledge.'

Whatever you are doing, however you may feel yourself—well, ill, good or bad tempered, nervous or confident—make sure the audience feels that you are enjoying yourself. And the best way to convey that impression *is* to enjoy yourself.

HM The Queen Mother talking to the author at the Royal Concert in aid of the Musicians Benevolent Fund, whose Chairman, Sir Thomas Armstrong, is in the right foreground with Imogen Holst. HRH The Duchess of Gloucester is talking to John Morton, General Secretary of the Musicians' Union and Susan Alcock, General Secretary of the Incorporated Society of Musicians.

POSTSCRIPT

THE MUSICIANS BENEVOLENT FUND

Any professional musician who falls on hard times should get in touch with the Musicians Benevolent Fund. The Fund exists to help all categories of professional musicians, young and old, in times of sickness, distress and need of any kind. Many musicians are too shy or modest to seek assistance; some are too proud. But this is the musicians own charity, and the Musicians Benevolent Fund welcomes information directly, or through friends, about anyone in need.

It also welcomes contributions from musicians who are doing well and enjoying success in their careers.

MUSICIANS BENEVOLENT FUND
St Cecilia House, 16 Ogle Street, London W1P 7LG,
Telephone 01-636 4481

APPENDIX I

Specialist Schools and Schools Offering Scholarships and Special Music Facilities

Pimlico Comprehensive School, London SW1.
Purcell School, Harrow on the Hill, Middx.
Chetham's Hospital School of Music, Manchester, Lancs.
Manchester High School of Art, Manchester, Lancs.
Minster Grammar School, Southwell, Notts.
St Mary's School, Edinburgh, Lothian.
Yehudi Menuhin School, Stoke D'Abernon, Surrey.
Wells Cathedral Music School, Wells, Somerset.

*   *   *   *   *

Abbotsholme School, Uttoxeter, Staffs.
Aldenham School, Elstree, Herts.
Abbey School, Malvern Wells, Hereford & Worcs.
Allhallows School, Rousden, Dorset.
Ampleforth College, York, Yorks.
Alan Angus, Haywards Heath, Sussex.
Badminton School, Bristol, Avon.
Bearwood College, Wokingham, Berks.
Bedales School, Petersfield, Hants.
Bedford School, Bedford, Beds.
Bembridge School, Bembridge, Isle of Wight.
Bethany School, Cranbrook, Kent.
Bishop's Stortford College, Bishop's Stortford, Herts.
Bloxham School, Bloxham, Oxon.
Blundell's School, Tiverton, Devon.
Bradfield College, Reading, Berks.
Brighton College, Brighton, Sussex.
Bromsgrove School, Bromsgrove, Worcs.
Bryanston School, Blandford Forum, Dorset.
Campbell College, Belfast, Northern Ireland
Canford School, Wimborne, Dorset.
Convent of Our Lady, St Leonards on Sea, Sussex.
Charterhouse, Godalming, Surrey.

Cheltenham College, Cheltenham, Glos.
Christ College, Brecon, Powys.
City of London School, London EC4.
Clayesmore School, Blandford Forum, Dorset.
Clifton College, Bristol, Avon.
Clifton High School for Girls, Bristol, Avon.
Cranbrook School, Cranbrook, Kent.
Cranleigh School, Cranleigh, Surrey.
Croft House School, Blandford Forum, Dorset.
Dean Close School, Cheltenham, Glos.
Denstone College, Uttoxeter, Staffs.
Dover College, Dover, Kent.
Downe House, Newbury, Berks.
Dulwich College, London SE21.
Durham School, Durham City, Co. Durham.
Eastbourne College. Eastbourne, Sussex.
Ellesmere College, Ellesmere, Salop.
Epsom College, Epsom, Surrey.
Eton College, Eton, Berks.
Felixstowe College, Felixstowe, Suffolk.
Felsted School, Dunmow, Essex.
Forest School, London E17.
Framlingham College, Woodbridge, Suffolk.
Giggleswick School, Settle, Yorks.
Gordonstoun School, Elgin, Morayshire.
Goudhurst College, Nantwich, Cheshire.
Great Walstead School, Lindfield, Sussex.
Gresham's School, Holt, Norfolk.
Haileybury, Hertford, Herts.
Highgate School, London N6.
Hollington Park School, St Leonards on Sea, Sussex.
Howell's School, Denbigh, Clwyd.
Hurstpierpoint College, Hassocks, Sussex.
Ipswich School, Ipswich, Suffolk.
Kelly College, Tavistock, Devon.
Kingham Hall School, Oxford, Oxon.
King's College, Taunton, Somerset.
King's School, Bruton, Somerset.
King's School, Canterbury, Kent.
King's School, Ely, Cambs.
King's School, Rochester, Kent.
King's School, Worcester, Worcs.
King William's College, Castletown, Isle of Man.
Lancing College, Lancing, Sussex.
Leeds Grammar School, Leeds, Yorks.
Leighton Park School, Reading, Berks.
Leys School, Cambridge, Cambs.

Lord Wandsworth College, Basingstoke, Hants.
Loretto School, Musselburgh, Midlothian.
Malvern College, Malvern, Worcs.
Malvern Girls College, Malvern, Worcs.
Malborough College, Marlborough, Wilts.
Merchant Taylors' School, Northwood, Middx.
Millfield School, Street, Somerset.
Mill Hill School, London NW7.
Milton Abbey School, Blandford Forum, Dorset.
Monkton Combe School, Nr Bath, Somerset.
Oakham School, Oakham, Leics.
Oratory School, Nr Reading, Berks.
Oundle School, Peterborough, Northants.
Pangbourne College, Pangbourne, Berks.
Pocklington School, Pocklington, Yorks.
Queen Ethelburga's School, Harrogate, N. Yorks.
Queenswood, Hatfield, Herts.
Radley College, Abingdon, Oxon.
Redrice School, Nr Andover, Hants.
Rehdcomb College, Nr Cirencester, Glos.
Repton School, Derby, Derbyshire.
Ringwood Grammar, Bournemouth, Hants.
Rossall School, Fleetwood, Lancs.
Rugby School, Rugby, Warks.
Rydal School, Colwyn Bay, Clwyd.
St Audrie's School, West Quantoxhead, Somerset.
St Bees School, St Bees, Cumbria.
St Brandon's School, Clevedon, Avon.
St Edmund's College, Ware, Herts.
St Edmund's School, Canterbury, Kent.
St Edward's College, Liverpool, Lancs.
St Edward's School, Oxford, Oxon.
St John's School, Leatherhead, Surrey.
St Lawrence College, Ramsgate, Kent.
St Leonard's School, St Andrews, Fife.
St Paul's Girls School, London W6.
St Paul's School, London SW13.
Scarborough College, Scarborough, Yorks.
Seaford College, Petworth, W. Sussex.
Sedbergh School, Sedbergh, Cumbria.
Sherborne School, Sherborne, Dorset.
Sherborne School for Girls, Sherborne, Dorset.
Shrewsbury School, Shrewsbury, Shropshire.
Solihull School, Solihull, Warks.
Stonyhurst College, Nr Blackburn, Lancs.
Stowe School, Buckingham, Bucks.
Strathallan School, Fordagenny, Perth.

Sutton Valence School, Maidstone, Kent.
Taunton School, Taunton, Somerset.
Tettenhall College, Wolverhampton, W. Midlands.
Tonbridge School, Tonbridge, Kent.
Trent College, Long Eaton, Nottingham, Notts.
Trinity College, Glenalmond, Perthshire.
Trinity School of John Whitgift, Croydon, London.
Truro School, Truro, Cornwall.
Uppingham School, Uppingham, Leics.
Wellingborough School, Wellingborough, Northants.
Willington College, Crowthorne, Berks.
Westminster School, London SW1.
Westonbirt School, Tetbury, Glos.
Whitgift School, Haling Park, South Croydon, London.
Winchester College, Winchester, Hants.
Worksop College, Worksop, Notts.
Wrekin College, Telford, Salop.
Wycliffe College, Stonehouse, Glos.
Wycombe Abbey, High Wycombe, Bucks.
Department of Education & Science, Guildford, Surrey.
London Schools Music Association, London E1.
National Association for Gifted Children, London W1.

APPENDIX 2

Youth Orchestras

The major Youth Orchestras in Britain are:

British Youth Symphony Orchestra;
British Youth Wind Orchestra;
National Youth Brass Band of Scotland;
National Youth Orchestra of Great Britain;
National Youth Orchestra of Wales;
National Youth String Orchestra of Scotland;
National Youth Wind Band of Scotland;
European Community Youth Orchestra.

In addition there are Regional and Local Youth Orchestras in most parts of the country, the addresses of which can be obtained from the offices of Local Education Authorities.

Information about many aspects of music in education and associated activities can be obtained from H. M. Inspector of Music, Mr I. P. Salisbury, Gateway House, 86 Northgate Street, Chester CH1 2HT.

APPENDIX 3

Pre-College Music Courses

Boston College of Further Education, Lincs.
Bromsgrove College of Further Education, Worcs.
Cambridge College of Arts and Technology, Cambs.
Cardiff College of Technology, Wales.
Chelmsford Technical College and School of Art, Essex.
Chiswick Music Centre, London.
Colchester Technical College and School of Art, Essex.
Coventry School of Music, Warks.
Dartington College of Arts, Devon.
Durham Technical College, Co. Durham.
Edinburgh College of Commerce, Lothian.
Hendon College of Technology, Middlesex.
Hitchin College of Further Education, Herts.
Huddersfield Polytechnic, Yorks.
Kingsway College of Further Education, London.
Mabel Fletcher Technical College, Liverpool, Merseyside.
Mid-Warwick College of Further Education, Leamington Spa, Warks.
Winchester School of Art, Hants.

APPENDIX 4

Colleges of Music

The main colleges of music are:

Birmingham School of Music, City of Birmingham Polytechnic, Birmingham, W. Midlands.
Guildhall School of Music and Drama, Barbican, London EC4.
London College of Music, Gt Marlborough St, London W1.
Royal Academy of Music, Marylebone Rd, London NW1.
Royal College of Music, Prince Consort Rd, London SW7.
Royal Northern College of Music, Oxford Rd, Manchester, Lancs.
Royal Scottish Academy of Music and Drama, St George's Pl., Glasgow, Strathclyde.
Trinity College of Music, Mandeville Pl., London W1.
Welsh College of Music and Drama, Castle Grounds, Cardiff, S. Glamorgan.

There are many other schools of music in different parts of the country the most notable of which are:

Belfast Academy of Music and Drama, Belfast, N. Ireland.
Colchester Institute of Higher Education, Colchester, Essex.
Dartington College of Arts, Totnes, Devon.
Huddersfield School of Music, Queensgate, Huddersfield, Yorks.
Newton Park College, Bath, Somerset.

APPENDIX 5

Universities Offering Degrees in Music

Aberdeen
Belfast
Birmingham
Bristol
Cambridge
Durham
East Anglia
　　Earlham Hall, Norwich
Edinburgh
Exeter
Glasgow
Hull
Keele
Lancaster
Leeds
Leicester
Liverpool
London
　　Goldsmiths College, SE14.
　　Kings College, Strand, WC2.
　　Royal Holloway College,
　　　　Egham, Surrey.
　　School of Oriental & African Studies,
　　　　Malet Street, WC1.

London (City of), St John Street, EC1.
Manchester
Newcastle-upon-Tyne
Nottingham
Open University, Walton Hall,
　　Milton Keynes
Oxford
Reading
St Andrews
Salford
Sheffield
Southampton
Surrey, Guildford
Sussex, Falmer, Brighton
Wales
　　College of Wales, Aberystwyth
　　College of North Wales, Bangor
　　University College, Cardiff
York

APPENDIX 6

Regional Arts Associations

Eastern Arts Assoc., 30 Station Rd, Cambridge.
East Midlands Arts Assoc., 1 Frederick St, Loughborough.
Greater London Arts Assoc., 25/31 Tavistock Pl., London WC1.
Lincolnshire and Humberside Arts Assoc., Beaumont Fee, Lincoln.
Merseyside Arts Assoc., School La., Liverpool.
North Wales Assoc. for the Arts, 10 Wellfield House, Bangor.
Northern Arts, 31 New Bridge St, Newcastle-upon-Tyne.
North West Arts, 52 King St, Manchester.
South East Arts Assoc., 58 London Rd, Tonbridge Wells.
South East Wales Arts Assoc., Victoria St, Cwmbran.
Southern Arts Assoc., 19 Southgate St, Winchester.
South West Arts, 23 Southernhay East, Devon.
West Midlands Arts, Market St, Stafford.
West Wales Assoc. for the Arts, Red St, Carmarthen.
Yorkshire Arts Assoc., Glydegate, Bradford.

APPENDIX 7

Artists' Agents

There are many agents in the field of management and promotion and there are always plenty of newcomers to this very interesting area of musical activity, some ephemerally or with very limited range of activity. The list given here is necessarily limited to a selection of the principal established agents.

AIM (Artists International Management Ltd), 5 Regents Park, NW1.
Allied Artists Agency, 36 Beauchamp Pl., SW3.
Askonas (Lies), 19a Air St, Regent St, W1.
Coast (John), 1 Park Cl., SW1.
Gorlinsky (S.A.) Ltd, 35 Dover St, W1.
Harrison/Parrott Ltd, 22 Hillgate St, W8.
Harold Holt Ltd, 134 Wigmore St, W1.
Ibbs and Tillett, 124 Wigmore St, W1.
Ingpen and Williams Ltd, 14 Kensington Cl., W8.
Koos (G. de), 416 Kings Rd, SW10.
London Artists Ltd, 124 Wigmore St, W1.
McCann (Norman) Ltd, 19 Charing Cross Rd, WC2.
Slasberg Agency, 3 The Lodge, Richmond Way, W12.
Stafford Law Associates, 14a Station Av., Walton-on-Thames, Surrey.
Tower Music, 125 Tottenham Court Rd, W1.
Van Walsum Concert Management, 22a Burlington Av., Kew Gardens, Richmond.
Van Wyck (Wilfrid), Troon, Old Mill La., Bray, Maidenhead, Berks.

APPENDIX 8

Principal Recording Companies

Abbey Recording Co. Ltd, Abbey St, Eynsham, Oxford, Oxon.
Argo Record Co., 115 Fulham Rd, London SW3.
BBC Tapes and Records, The Langham, Portland Pl., London W1.
CBS Records Ltd, 28–30 Theobalds Rd, London WC1.
Classics for Pleasure, Astronaut House, 80 Blyth Rd, Hayes, Middx.
Decca Record Co Ltd, 9 Albert Embankment, London SE1.
EMI Records, 20 Manchester Sq., London W1.
Lyrita Recorded Edition, 99 Green La., Burnham, Slough, Berks.
Music for Pleasure Ltd, 80 Blyth Rd, Hayes, Middx.
Phonogram Ltd (Phillips), Stanhope House, Stanhope Pl., London W2.
Polydor Ltd (Deutshe Gramophon), 17–19 Stratford Pl., London W1.
Pye Records Ltd, 17 Gt Cumberland Pl., London W1.
RCA (Gt Britain) Ltd, 50 Curzon St, London W1.
Saga Records Ltd, 326 Kensal Rd, London W10.
Unicorn Records Ltd, Manor House, Wakefield Leicester, Leics.

APPENDIX 9

Principal Music Publishers

Music Publishers Association, 73/75 Mortimer St, London W1.
Ashdown, Edwin, & Co., 275/281 Cricklewood Broadway, London NW2.
Boosey & Hawkes, Regent St, London W1.
Bosworth, 14/18 Heddon St, London W1.
Chappell, 50 New Bond St, London W1.
J. & W. Chester Ltd, Eagle Ct., London EC1.
J.B. Cramer, 99 St Martins La., London WC2.
Elkin, William, Music Services, Deacon House, Brundall, Norfolk.
Faber Music, 38 Russell Sq., London WC1.
Hinrichsen Edition, 119/125 Wardour St, London W1.
Lenquick, Purley Oaks Studio, 421A Brighton Rd, South Croydon, Surrey.
Musica Rara, 2 Gt Marlborough St, London W1.
Novello & Co. Ltd, Borough Green, Sevenoaks, Kent.
   Showroom, 38a Beak St, London W1.
Oxford University Press, 44 Conduit St, London W1.
Paterson, 38 Wigmore St, London W1.
Ricordi (London) Ltd, 36 Wigmore St, London W1.
Schott, 48 Gt Marlborough St, London W1.
Stainer & Bell, 82 High Rd, London N2.
United Music Publishers, 1 Montagu St, London WC1.
Universal Edition, 2-3 Fareham St, London W1.
Joseph Weinberger, 10/16 Rathbone St, London W1.

APPENDIX 10

Professional Orchestras

Academy of St Martin in the Fields.
BBC Concert Orch., BBC, 156 Gt Portland St, London W1.
BBC Northern Ireland Orch., BBC, 25–7 Orman Av., Belfast.
BBC Northern Symph. Orch., BBC, PO Box 27, Manchester.
BBC Scottish Radio Orch., BBC, Queen Margaret Dr., Glasgow.
BBC Scottish Symph. Orch., BBC, Queen Margaret Dr., Glasgow.
BBC Symph. Orch., BBC, Gt Portland St, London W1.
BBC Welsh Orch., BBC, Llandaff, Cardiff.
Birmingham, City of, Symph. Orch., 60 Newhall St, Birmingham.
Bournemouth Sinfonietta, Westover Mansions, Gervis Pl., Bournemouth.
Bristol Sinfonia, 16 Foye House, Bridge Rd, Leigh Woods, Bristol.
Brighton Philharmonic Orch., 5 Bartholomews, Brighton.
English Chamber Orch., 1a Bloemfontein Way, London W12.
English National Opera Orch., London Coliseum, St Martins La., London WC2.
English Sinfonia, 72 St James's St, Nottingham.
Guildford Philharmonic, 155 High St, Guildford.
Hallé Orch., 30 Cross St, Manchester.
London Concert Orch., 125 Tottenham Ct Rd, London W1.
London Mozart Players, 105 Hartfield Rd, London SW19.
London Philharmonic Orch., 53 Welbeck St, London W1.
London Sinfonietta, Kingston Hill Pl., Kingston Hill, Surrey.
London Symph. Orch., 19/25 Argyll St, London W1.
Manchester Camerata, 19 Moorland Rd, Manchester.
Manchester Mozart Orch., Lancaster Farm, Longridge, Preston.
Menuhin Festival Orch., 134 Wigmore St, London W1.
New Symph. Orch., Suite 33, 20–21 Tooks Ct, London EC4.
Northern Sinfonia, 41 Jesmond Vale, Newcastle-upon-Tyne.
Philharmonia Orch. (previously New Philharmonia), 12 de Walden Ct, 85 New Cavendish St, London W1.
Philomusica of London, Suite 33, 20–21 Tooks Ct, London EC4.
Royal Liverpool Philharmonic Orch., Hope St, Liverpool.
Royal Opera House Orch., Royal Opera House, Covent Garden, London WC2.
Royal Philharmonic Orch., 97 New Bond St, London W1.
Scottish Baroque Ensemble, 14 Albany St, Edinburgh.
Scottish National Orch., 150 Hope St, Glasgow.

St John's, Smith Sq. Orch., 12 Elsworthy Rd, London NW3.
Ulster Orch., 181a Stranmillis Rd, Belfast.
Welsh Philharmonic Orch., Welsh National Opera Co., John St, Cardiff.

Staff and Regimental Bands of the British Army

HOUSEHOLD CAVALRY
The Life Guards*
The Blues and Royals* (Royal Horse Guards and 1st Dragoons)

ROYAL ARMOURED CORPS
1st The Queen's Dragoon Guards
The Royal Scots Dragoon Guards (Carabiniers and Greys)
4th/7th Royal Dragoon Guards
5th Royal Inniskilling Dragoon Guards
The Queen's Own Hussars
The Queen's Royal Irish Hussars
9th/12th Royal Lancers (Prince of Wales's)
The Royal Hussars (Prince of Wales's Own)
13th/18th Royal Hussars (Queen Mary's Own)
14th/20th King's Hussars
15th/19th The King's Royal Hussars
16th/5th The Queen's Royal Lancers
17th/21st Lancers

Royal Tank Regiment
(Three Staff Bands)
   Alamein
   Cambrai
   Rhine

ROYAL REGIMENT OF ARTILLERY
RA (Woolwich) Band
RA (Mounted) Band†
RA (Alanbrooke) Band

CORPS OF ROYAL ENGINEERS
RE (Chatham) Band
RE (Aldershot) Band

ROYAL CORPS OF SIGNALS
Band of The Royal Signals

GUARDS DIVISION
Grenadier Guards
Coldstream Guards
Scots Guards
Irish Guards
Welsh Guards

SCOTTISH DIVISION
The Royal Scots (The Royal Regiment)
The Royal Highland Fusiliers (Princess Margaret's Own Glasgow and Ayrshire Regiment)
The King's Own Scottish Borderers
The Black Watch (Royal Highland Regiment)
Queen's Own Highlanders (Seaforth and Camerons)
The Gordon Highlanders
The Argyll and Sutherland Highlanders (Princess Louise's)

QUEEN'S DIVISION
The Queen's Regiment
1st Battalion
2nd Battalion
3rd Battalion

The Royal Regiment of Fusiliers
1st Battalion
2nd Battalion
3rd Battalion

The Royal Anglian Regiment
1st Battalion
2nd Battalion
3rd Battalion

KING'S DIVISION
The King's Own Royal Border Regiment
The King's Regiment
The Prince of Wales's Own Regiment of Yorkshire
The Green Howards (Alexandra, Princess of Wales's Own Yorkshire Regiment)
The Royal Irish Rangers (27th (Inniskilling) 83rd and 87th)
    1st Battalion
    2nd Battalion
The Queen's Lancashire Regiment
The Duke of Wellington's Regiment (West Riding)

PRINCE OF WALES'S DIVISION
The Devonshire and Dorset Regiment
The Cheshire Regiment
The Royal Welch Fusiliers
The Royal Regiment of Wales (24th/41st Foot)

The Gloucestershire Regiment
The Worcestershire and Sherwood Foresters Regiment (29th/45th Foot)
The Royal Hampshire Regiment
The Staffordshire Regiment (The Prince of Wales's)
The Duke of Edinburgh's Royal Regiment (Berkshire and Wiltshire)

LIGHT DIVISION
The Light Infantry
1st Battalion
2nd Battalion
3rd Battalion

The Royal Green Jackets
1st Battalion
2nd Battalion
3rd Battalion

THE PARACHUTE REGIMENT
1st Battalion
2nd Battalion
3rd Battalion

ROYAL CORPS OF TRANSPORT
A Major Staff Band

ROYAL ARMY MEDICAL CORPS
A Staff Band

ROYAL ARMY ORDNANCE CORPS
A Staff Band

CORPS OF ROYAL ELECTRICAL AND MECHANICAL ENGINEERS
A Major Staff Band

ROYAL MILITARY ACADEMY SANDHURST BAND CORPS
A Staff Band

WOMEN'S ROYAL ARMY CORPS
A Staff Band

THE BRIGADE OF GURKHAS
The Band of the Brigade of Gurkhas (2nd King Edward VII's Own Gurkha Rifles)

Notes:
*This is a mounted Band   †This Band is no longer mounted

APPENDIX 12

Teacher Organisations

Association of Assistant Masters, 29 Gordon Sq., London WC1.
Association of Assistant Mistresses, 29 Gordon Sq., London WC1.
Association of Professional Singing Teachers, Festival Office, Aldeburgh, Suffolk.
Guild of Freelance Music Teachers, 16 Holwood Rd, Bromley, Kent.
Incorporated Association of Preparatory Schools, 138 Church St, London W8.
Incorporated Society of Musicians, 10 Stratford Pl., London W1.
Music Teachers Association, 106 Gloucester Pl., London W1.

APPENDIX 13

National Organisations

Arts Council of Great Britain, 105 Piccadilly, London W1V 0AU. 01-629 9495
Arts Council of Northern Ireland, 181a Stranmillis Rd, Belfast BT9 5DU. 0232 663591
Association of British Orchestras, 11 Little Britain, London EC1 7BX. 01-606 1507
British Actors Equity Association, 8 Harley St, London W1N 2AB. 01-636 6367
British Broadcasting Corporation, Broadcasting House, Gt Portland St, London W1A 1AA. 01-580 4468
  Music Division Radio: Yalding House, 156 Gt Portland St, London W1N 6AJ. 01-580 4468
  Television: Kensington House, Richmond Way, London W14 0AX. 01-743 1272
Belfast: Broadcasting House, Ormeau Av., Belfast BT2 8HQ. 0232 44400
Birmingham: Broadcasting Centre, Pebble Mill Rd, Birmingham B5 7QQ. 021-472 5253
Cardiff: Broadcasting House, Llandaff CF5 2YQ. 0222 564888
Glasgow: Broadcasting House, Queen Margaret Dr., Glasgow W2. 041-339 8844
Manchester: PO Box 27, Broadcasting House, Piccadilly, Manchester. 061-236 8444
British Council, 65 Davies St, London W1H 3DB. 01-935 6371
British Federation of Music Festivals, 106 Gloucester Pl., London W1H 3DB. 01-935 6371
British Music Information Centre, 10 Stratford Pl., London W1N 9AE. 01-499 8567
Composers Guild of Great Britain, 10 Stratford Pl., London W1N 9AE. 01-499 8567
Department of Education for Northern Ireland, Rathgael House, Balloo Rd., Bangor, Co. Down BT19 2PR. 0247 66311
Department of Education and Science (DES), Elizabeth House, York Rd, London SE1 7PH. 01-928 9222
Incorporated Society of Musicians, 10 Stratford Pl., London W1N 9AE. 01-629 4413
Independent Broadcasting Authority, 70 Brompton Rd, London SW3 1EY. 01-584 7011
London Orchestral Concerts Board, Royal Festival Hall, London SE1 8XX. 01-928 3641
Mechanical Copyright Protection Society, 380 Streatham High Rd, London SW16. 01-769 3181
Musicians Benevolent Fund, 16 Ogle St, London W1P 7LG. 01-636 4481
Musicians Union, 29 Catherine Pl., Buckingham Gate, London SW1E 6EH. 01-834 1348
Music Publishers Association, 73-75 Mortimer St, London W1N 7TB. 01-636 6027
National Federation of Music Societies, 1 Montagu St, London WC1B 5BF. 01-580 4885

National Music Council of Great Britain, 35 Morpeth Mansions, London SW1P 1EU.
  01-828 9691
National Union of Students Publications, 3 Endsleigh St, London WC1 0DU. 01-278
  3291
National Youth Orchestra of Great Britain, 94 Park Lane, Croydon, London CR0 1JB.
  01-686 6237
Performing Right Society Ltd, 29-33 Berners St, London W1P 4AA. 01-580 5544
Royal Society of Musicians of Great Britain, 10 Stratford Pl., London W1N 9AE. 01-
  629 6137
Rural Music Schools Association, Little Benslow Hills, Hitchin, Herts. 0462 59446
Scottish Arts Council, 19 Charlotte Sq., Edinburgh EH2 4DF. 031-226 6051
Scottish Education Department, St Andrews House, Edinburgh EH1 3DB. 031-556
  8501
Welsh Arts Council, 9 Museum Pl., Cardiff CF1 3NX. 0222 394711
Welsh Education Office, 31 Cathedral Rd, Cardiff CF1 9HB. 0222 42661
Worshipful Company of Musicians, 4 St Paul's Churchyard, London EC4M 8AY. 01-
  236 2333
Youth and Music, 22 Blomfield St, London EC2M 7AP. 01-628 0152

Bibliography

REFERENCE BOOKS

Arts Council Annual Report
British Music Year Book
Competitions, Awards and Scholarships for Music Students (Arts Council of Great Britain)
Education Charities (National Union of Students) publications
Groves Dictionary of Music and Musicians
International Who's Who in Music
Music publishers' catalogues giving instrumentation and duration of works
National Federation of Music Societies, handbook of members
Oxford Companion to Music (Scholes)

Timings of orchestral works have quite a wide variation subject to the conductors, soloists and orchestras involved, but there is a useful guide to average timings of the main repertoire in:
Aronowitz, *Performing Timings of Orchestral Works* (Ernest Benn)

Two invaluable items, collectors pieces and hard to come by:
BBC Radio list of works broadcast (compiled annually until 1970);
The Edwin Fleischer Collection Catalogue (with timings, instrumentations and dates of first performances)

PERIODICALS

Many of the periodicals listed below are available on Bookstalls otherwise they may be ordered from newsagents or music dealers.

Classical Music Weekly
The Composer
The Gramophone
Musical Opinion
Musical Times
Music and Musicians
Music in Education

Music Teacher
Music Week
Opera
Records and Recording
The Stage
The Strad

The Saturday edition of *The Times, Daily Telegraph,* and *Guardian* and the *Sunday Times, Observer* and *Sunday Telegraph* give lists of concerts and of appointments vacant for musicians and administrators. Of these the Saturday *Daily Telegraph* is usually the most comprehensive. *The Times Educational Supplement* is essential reading for music teachers in schools, colleges and universities.

Index